*Dedicated to all. And yes, **all** believers of the doctrine of free will. May this book be a guiding light and beacon of hope. In a hopeless world.*

-John C. Luther

Table Of Index

Man's Free Will

Whosoever.	Whosoever.	Whosoever.	Whosoever.
Whosoever.	Whosoever.	Whosoever.	Whosoever.
Whosoever.	Whosoever.	Whosoever.	Whosoever.
Whosoever.	Whosoever.	Whosoever.	Whosoever.
Whosoever.	Whosoever.	Whosoever.	Whosoever.
Whosoever.	Whosoever.	Whosoever.	Whosoever.
Whosoever.	Whosoever.	Whosoever.	Whosoever.
Whosoever.	Whosoever.	Whosoever.	Whosoever.
Whosoever.	Whosoever.	Whosoever.	Whosoever.
Whosoever.	Whosoever.	Whosoever.	Whosoever.
Whosoever.	Whosoever.	Whosoever.	Whosoever.
Whosoever.	Whosoever.	Whosoever.	Whosoever.
Whosoever.	Whosoever.	Whosoever.	Whosoever.
Whosoever.	Whosoever.	Whosoever.	Whosoever.
Whosoever.	Whosoever.	Whosoever.	Whosoever.
Whosoever.	Whosoever.	Whosoever.	Whosoever.
Whosoever.	Whosoever.	Whosoever.	Whosoever.
Whosoever.	Whosoever.	Whosoever.	Whosoever.
Whosoever.	Whosoever.	Whosoever.	Whosoever.
Whosoever.	Whosoever.	Whosoever.	Whosoever.
Whosoever.	Whosoever.	Whosoever.	Whosoever.
Whosoever.	Whosoever.	Whosoever.	Whosoever.
Whosoever.	Whosoever.	Whosoever.	Whosoever.
Whosoever.	Whosoever.	Whosoever.	Whosoever.
Whosoever.	Whosoever.	Whosoever.	Whosoever.
Whosoever.	Whosoever.	Whosoever.	Whosoever.
Whosoever.	Whosoever.	Whosoever.	Whosoever.

Whosoever. Whosoever. Whosoever. Whosoever.
Whosoever. Whosoever. Whosoever. Whosoever.
Whosoever. Whosoever. Whosoever. Whosoever.
Whosoever. Whosoever. Whosoever. Whosoever.
Whosoever. Whosoever. Whosoever. Whosoever.
Whosoever. Whosoever. Whosoever. Whosoever.
Whosoever. Whosoever. Whosoever. Whosoever.
Whosoever. Whosoever. Whosoever. Whosoever.
Whosoever. Whosoever. Whosoever. Whosoever.
Whosoever. Whosoever. Whosoever. Whosoever.
Whosoever. Whosoever. Whosoever. Whosoever.
Whosoever. Whosoever. Whosoever. Whosoever.
Whosoever. Whosoever. Whosoever. Whosoever.
Whosoever. Whosoever. Whosoever. Whosoever.
Whosoever. Whosoever. Whosoever. Whosoever.
Whosoever. Whosoever. Whosoever. Whosoever.
Whosoever. Whosoever. Whosoever. Whosoever.
Whosoever. Whosoever. Whosoever. Whosoever.
Whosoever. Whosoever. Whosoever. Whosoever.
Whosoever. Whosoever. Whosoever. Whosoever.
Whosoever. Whosoever. Whosoever. Whosoever.
Whosoever. Whosoever. Whosoever. Whosoever.
Whosoever. Whosoever. Whosoever. Whosoever.
Whosoever. Whosoever. Whosoever. Whosoever.
Whosoever. Whosoever. Whosoever. Whosoever.
Whosoever. Whosoever. Whosoever. Whosoever.
Whosoever. Whosoever. Whosoever. Whosoever.
Whosoever. Whosoever. Whosoever. Whosoever.
Whosoever. Whosoever. Whosoever. Whosoever.
Whosoever. Whosoever. Whosoever. Whosoever.

Whosoever.	Whosoever.	Whosoever.	Whosoever.
Whosoever.	Whosoever.	Whosoever.	Whosoever.
Whosoever.	Whosoever.	Whosoever.	Whosoever.
Whosoever.	Whosoever.	Whosoever.	Whosoever.
Whosoever.	Whosoever.	Whosoever.	Whosoever.
Whosoever.	Whosoever.	Whosoever.	Whosoever.
Whosoever.	Whosoever.	Whosoever.	Whosoever.
Whosoever.	Whosoever.	Whosoever.	Whosoever.
Whosoever.	Whosoever.	Whosoever.	Whosoever.
Whosoever.	Whosoever.	Whosoever.	Whosoever.
Whosoever.	Whosoever.	Whosoever.	Whosoever.
Whosoever.	Whosoever.	Whosoever.	Whosoever.
Whosoever.	Whosoever.	Whosoever.	Whosoever.
Whosoever.	Whosoever.	Whosoever.	Whosoever.
Whosoever.	Whosoever.	Whosoever.	Whosoever.
Whosoever.	Whosoever.	Whosoever.	Whosoever.
Whosoever.	Whosoever.	Whosoever.	Whosoever.
Whosoever.	Whosoever.	Whosoever.	Whosoever.
Whosoever.	Whosoever.	Whosoever.	Whosoever.
Whosoever.	Whosoever.	Whosoever.	Whosoever.
Whosoever.	Whosoever.	Whosoever.	Whosoever.
Whosoever.	Whosoever.	Whosoever.	Whosoever.
Whosoever.	Whosoever.	Whosoever.	Whosoever.
Whosoever.	Whosoever.	Whosoever.	Whosoever.
Whosoever.	Whosoever.	Whosoever.	Whosoever.
Whosoever.	Whosoever.	Whosoever.	Whosoever.
Whosoever.	Whosoever.	Whosoever.	Whosoever.
Whosoever.	Whosoever.	Whosoever.	Whosoever.

Whosoever.	Whosoever.	Whosoever.	Whosoever.
Whosoever.	Whosoever.	Whosoever.	Whosoever.
Whosoever.	Whosoever.	Whosoever.	Whosoever.
Whosoever.	Whosoever.	Whosoever.	Whosoever.
Whosoever.	Whosoever.	Whosoever.	Whosoever.
Whosoever.	Whosoever.	Whosoever.	Whosoever.
Whosoever.	Whosoever.	Whosoever.	Whosoever.
Whosoever.	Whosoever.	Whosoever.	Whosoever.
Whosoever.	Whosoever.	Whosoever.	Whosoever.
Whosoever.	Whosoever.	Whosoever.	Whosoever.
Whosoever.	Whosoever.	Whosoever.	Whosoever.
Whosoever.	Whosoever.	Whosoever.	Whosoever.
Whosoever.	Whosoever.	Whosoever.	Whosoever.
Whosoever.	Whosoever.	Whosoever.	Whosoever.
Whosoever.	Whosoever.	Whosoever.	Whosoever.
Whosoever.	Whosoever.	Whosoever.	Whosoever.
Whosoever.	Whosoever.	Whosoever.	Whosoever.
Whosoever.	Whosoever.	Whosoever.	Whosoever.
Whosoever.	Whosoever.	Whosoever.	Whosoever.
Whosoever.	Whosoever.	Whosoever.	Whosoever.
Whosoever.	Whosoever.	Whosoever.	Whosoever.
Whosoever.	Whosoever.	Whosoever.	Whosoever.
Whosoever.	Whosoever.	Whosoever.	Whosoever.
Whosoever.	Whosoever.	Whosoever.	Whosoever.
Whosoever.	Whosoever.	Whosoever.	Whosoever.
Whosoever.	Whosoever.	Whosoever.	Whosoever.
Whosoever.	Whosoever.	Whosoever.	Whosoever.

Whosoever.	Whosoever.	Whosoever.	Whosoever.
Whosoever.	Whosoever.	Whosoever.	Whosoever.
Whosoever.	Whosoever.	Whosoever.	Whosoever.
Whosoever.	Whosoever.	Whosoever.	Whosoever.
Whosoever.	Whosoever.	Whosoever.	Whosoever.
Whosoever.	Whosoever.	Whosoever.	Whosoever.
Whosoever.	Whosoever.	Whosoever.	Whosoever.
Whosoever.	Whosoever.	Whosoever.	Whosoever.
Whosoever.	Whosoever.	Whosoever.	Whosoever.
Whosoever.	Whosoever.	Whosoever.	Whosoever.
Whosoever.	Whosoever.	Whosoever.	Whosoever.
Whosoever.	Whosoever.	Whosoever.	Whosoever.
Whosoever.	Whosoever.	Whosoever.	Whosoever.
Whosoever.	Whosoever.	Whosoever.	Whosoever.
Whosoever.	Whosoever.	Whosoever.	Whosoever.
Whosoever.	Whosoever.	Whosoever.	Whosoever.
Whosoever.	Whosoever.	Whosoever.	Whosoever.
Whosoever.	Whosoever.	Whosoever.	Whosoever.
Whosoever.	Whosoever.	Whosoever.	Whosoever.
Whosoever.	Whosoever.	Whosoever.	Whosoever.
Whosoever.	Whosoever.	Whosoever.	Whosoever.
Whosoever.	Whosoever.	Whosoever.	Whosoever.
Whosoever.	Whosoever.	Whosoever.	Whosoever.
Whosoever.	Whosoever.	Whosoever.	Whosoever.
Whosoever.	Whosoever.	Whosoever.	Whosoever.

Whosoever.	Whosoever.	Whosoever.	Whosoever.
Whosoever.	Whosoever.	Whosoever.	Whosoever.
Whosoever.	Whosoever.	Whosoever.	Whosoever.
Whosoever.	Whosoever.	Whosoever.	Whosoever.
Whosoever.	Whosoever.	Whosoever.	Whosoever.
Whosoever.	Whosoever.	Whosoever.	Whosoever.
Whosoever.	Whosoever.	Whosoever.	Whosoever.
Whosoever.	Whosoever.	Whosoever.	Whosoever.
Whosoever.	Whosoever.	Whosoever.	Whosoever.
Whosoever.	Whosoever.	Whosoever.	Whosoever.
Whosoever.	Whosoever.	Whosoever.	Whosoever.
Whosoever.	Whosoever.	Whosoever.	Whosoever.
Whosoever.	Whosoever.	Whosoever.	Whosoever.
Whosoever.	Whosoever.	Whosoever.	Whosoever.
Whosoever.	Whosoever.	Whosoever.	Whosoever.
Whosoever.	Whosoever.	Whosoever.	Whosoever.
Whosoever.	Whosoever.	Whosoever.	Whosoever.
Whosoever.	Whosoever.	Whosoever.	Whosoever.
Whosoever.	Whosoever.	Whosoever.	Whosoever.
Whosoever.	Whosoever.	Whosoever.	Whosoever.
Whosoever.	Whosoever.	Whosoever.	Whosoever.
Whosoever.	Whosoever.	Whosoever.	Whosoever.
Whosoever.	Whosoever.	Whosoever.	Whosoever.
Whosoever.	Whosoever.	Whosoever.	Whosoever.
Whosoever.	Whosoever.	Whosoever.	Whosoever.
Whosoever.	Whosoever.	Whosoever.	Whosoever.
Whosoever.	Whosoever.	Whosoever.	Whosoever.

Whosoever. Whosoever. Whosoever. Whosoever.
Whosoever. Whosoever. Whosoever. Whosoever.
Whosoever. Whosoever. Whosoever. Whosoever.
Whosoever. Whosoever. Whosoever. Whosoever.
Whosoever. Whosoever. Whosoever. Whosoever.
Whosoever. Whosoever. Whosoever. Whosoever.
Whosoever. Whosoever. Whosoever. Whosoever.
Whosoever. Whosoever. Whosoever. Whosoever.
Whosoever. Whosoever. Whosoever. Whosoever.
Whosoever. Whosoever. Whosoever. Whosoever.
Whosoever. Whosoever. Whosoever. Whosoever.
Whosoever. Whosoever. Whosoever. Whosoever.
Whosoever. Whosoever. Whosoever. Whosoever.
Whosoever. Whosoever. Whosoever. Whosoever.
Whosoever. Whosoever. Whosoever. Whosoever.
Whosoever. Whosoever. Whosoever. Whosoever.
Whosoever. Whosoever. Whosoever. Whosoever.
Whosoever. Whosoever. Whosoever. Whosoever.
Whosoever. Whosoever. Whosoever. Whosoever.
Whosoever. Whosoever. Whosoever. Whosoever.
Whosoever. Whosoever. Whosoever. Whosoever.
Whosoever. Whosoever. Whosoever. Whosoever.
Whosoever. Whosoever. Whosoever. Whosoever.
Whosoever. Whosoever. Whosoever. Whosoever.
Whosoever. Whosoever. Whosoever. Whosoever.
Whosoever. Whosoever. Whosoever. Whosoever.
Whosoever. Whosoever. Whosoever. Whosoever.
Whosoever. Whosoever. Whosoever. Whosoever.

Whosoever. Whosoever. Whosoever. Whosoever.
Whosoever. Whosoever. Whosoever. Whosoever.
Whosoever. Whosoever. Whosoever. Whosoever.
Whosoever. Whosoever. Whosoever. Whosoever.
Whosoever. Whosoever. Whosoever. Whosoever.
Whosoever. Whosoever. Whosoever. Whosoever.
Whosoever. Whosoever. Whosoever. Whosoever.
Whosoever. Whosoever. Whosoever. Whosoever.
Whosoever. Whosoever. Whosoever. Whosoever.
Whosoever. Whosoever. Whosoever. Whosoever.
Whosoever. Whosoever. Whosoever. Whosoever.
Whosoever. Whosoever. Whosoever. Whosoever.
Whosoever. Whosoever. Whosoever. Whosoever.
Whosoever. Whosoever. Whosoever. Whosoever.
Whosoever. Whosoever. Whosoever. Whosoever.
Whosoever. Whosoever. Whosoever. Whosoever.
Whosoever. Whosoever. Whosoever. Whosoever.
Whosoever. Whosoever. Whosoever. Whosoever.
Whosoever. Whosoever. Whosoever. Whosoever.
Whosoever. Whosoever. Whosoever. Whosoever.
Whosoever. Whosoever. Whosoever. Whosoever.
Whosoever. Whosoever. Whosoever. Whosoever.
Whosoever. Whosoever. Whosoever. Whosoever.
Whosoever. Whosoever. Whosoever. Whosoever.
Whosoever. Whosoever. Whosoever. Whosoever

Whosoever. Whosoever. Whosoever. Whosoever.
Whosoever. Whosoever. Whosoever. Whosoever.
Whosoever. Whosoever. Whosoever. Whosoever.
Whosoever. Whosoever. Whosoever. Whosoever.
Whosoever. Whosoever. Whosoever. Whosoever.
Whosoever. Whosoever. Whosoever. Whosoever.
Whosoever. Whosoever. Whosoever. Whosoever.
Whosoever. Whosoever. Whosoever. Whosoever.
Whosoever. Whosoever. Whosoever. Whosoever.
Whosoever. Whosoever. Whosoever. Whosoever.
Whosoever. Whosoever. Whosoever. Whosoever.
Whosoever. Whosoever. Whosoever. Whosoever.
Whosoever. Whosoever. Whosoever. Whosoever.
Whosoever. Whosoever. Whosoever. Whosoever.
Whosoever. Whosoever. Whosoever. Whosoever.
Whosoever. Whosoever. Whosoever. Whosoever.
Whosoever. Whosoever. Whosoever. Whosoever.
Whosoever. Whosoever. Whosoever. Whosoever.
Whosoever. Whosoever. Whosoever. Whosoever.
Whosoever. Whosoever. Whosoever. Whosoever.
Whosoever. Whosoever. Whosoever. Whosoever.
Whosoever. Whosoever. Whosoever. Whosoever.
Whosoever. Whosoever. Whosoever. Whosoever.
Whosoever. Whosoever. Whosoever. Whosoever.
Whosoever. Whosoever. Whosoever. Whosoever.

Whosoever.	Whosoever.	Whosoever.	Whosoever.
Whosoever.	Whosoever.	Whosoever.	Whosoever.
Whosoever.	Whosoever.	Whosoever.	Whosoever.
Whosoever.	Whosoever.	Whosoever.	Whosoever.
Whosoever.	Whosoever.	Whosoever.	Whosoever.
Whosoever.	Whosoever.	Whosoever.	Whosoever.
Whosoever.	Whosoever.	Whosoever.	Whosoever.
Whosoever.	Whosoever.	Whosoever.	Whosoever.
Whosoever.	Whosoever.	Whosoever.	Whosoever.
Whosoever.	Whosoever.	Whosoever.	Whosoever.
Whosoever.	Whosoever.	Whosoever.	Whosoever.
Whosoever.	Whosoever.	Whosoever.	Whosoever.
Whosoever.	Whosoever.	Whosoever.	Whosoever.
Whosoever.	Whosoever.	Whosoever.	Whosoever.
Whosoever.	Whosoever.	Whosoever.	Whosoever.
Whosoever.	Whosoever.	Whosoever.	Whosoever.
Whosoever.	Whosoever.	Whosoever.	Whosoever.
Whosoever.	Whosoever.	Whosoever.	Whosoever.
Whosoever.	Whosoever.	Whosoever.	Whosoever.
Whosoever.	Whosoever.	Whosoever.	Whosoever.
Whosoever.	Whosoever.	Whosoever.	Whosoever.
Whosoever.	Whosoever.	Whosoever.	Whosoever.
Whosoever.	Whosoever.	Whosoever.	Whosoever.
Whosoever.	Whosoever.	Whosoever.	Whosoever.
Whosoever.	Whosoever.	Whosoever.	Whosoever.
Whosoever.	Whosoever.	Whosoever.	Whosoever.
Whosoever.	Whosoever.	Whosoever.	Whosoever.

Whosoever.	Whosoever.	Whosoever.	Whosoever.
Whosoever.	Whosoever.	Whosoever.	Whosoever.
Whosoever.	Whosoever.	Whosoever.	Whosoever.
Whosoever.	Whosoever.	Whosoever.	Whosoever.
Whosoever.	Whosoever.	Whosoever.	Whosoever.
Whosoever.	Whosoever.	Whosoever.	Whosoever.
Whosoever.	Whosoever.	Whosoever.	Whosoever.
Whosoever.	Whosoever.	Whosoever.	Whosoever.
Whosoever.	Whosoever.	Whosoever.	Whosoever.
Whosoever.	Whosoever.	Whosoever.	Whosoever.
Whosoever.	Whosoever.	Whosoever.	Whosoever.
Whosoever.	Whosoever.	Whosoever.	Whosoever.
Whosoever.	Whosoever.	Whosoever.	Whosoever.
Whosoever.	Whosoever.	Whosoever.	Whosoever.
Whosoever.	Whosoever.	Whosoever.	Whosoever.
Whosoever.	Whosoever.	Whosoever.	Whosoever.
Whosoever.	Whosoever.	Whosoever.	Whosoever.
Whosoever.	Whosoever.	Whosoever.	Whosoever.
Whosoever.	Whosoever.	Whosoever.	Whosoever.
Whosoever.	Whosoever.	Whosoever.	Whosoever.
Whosoever.	Whosoever.	Whosoever.	Whosoever.
Whosoever.	Whosoever.	Whosoever.	Whosoever.
Whosoever.	Whosoever.	Whosoever.	Whosoever.
Whosoever.	Whosoever.	Whosoever.	Whosoever.
Whosoever.	Whosoever.	Whosoever.	Whosoever.
Whosoever.	Whosoever.	Whosoever.	Whosoever.
Whosoever.	Whosoever.	Whosoever.	Whosoever.
Whosoever.	Whosoever.	Whosoever.	Whosoever.
Whosoever.	Whosoever.	Whosoever.	Whosoever.

But, God Is Love???

John 3:16	John 3:16	John 3:16	John 3:16
John 3:16	John 3:16	John 3:16	John 3:16
John 3:16	John 3:16	John 3:16	John 3:16
John 3:16	John 3:16	John 3:16	John 3:16
John 3:16	John 3:16	John 3:16	John 3:16
John 3:16	John 3:16	John 3:16	John 3:16
John 3:16	John 3:16	John 3:16	John 3:16
John 3:16	John 3:16	John 3:16	John 3:16
John 3:16	John 3:16	John 3:16	John 3:16
John 3:16	John 3:16	John 3:16	John 3:16
John 3:16	John 3:16	John 3:16	John 3:16
John 3:16	John 3:16	John 3:16	John 3:16
John 3:16	John 3:16	John 3:16	John 3:16
John 3:16	John 3:16	John 3:16	John 3:16
John 3:16	John 3:16	John 3:16	John 3:16
John 3:16	John 3:16	John 3:16	John 3:16
John 3:16	John 3:16	John 3:16	John 3:16
John 3:16	John 3:16	John 3:16	John 3:16
John 3:16	John 3:16	John 3:16	John 3:16
John 3:16	John 3:16	John 3:16	John 3:16
John 3:16	John 3:16	John 3:16	John 3:16
John 3:16	John 3:16	John 3:16	John 3:16
John 3:16	John 3:16	John 3:16	John 3:16
John 3:16	John 3:16	John 3:16	John 3:16
John 3:16	John 3:16	John 3:16	John 3:16
John 3:16	John 3:16	John 3:16	John 3:16
John 3:16	John 3:16	John 3:16	John 3:16

John 3:16 John 3:16 John 3:16 John 3:16
John 3:16 John 3:16 John 3:16 John 3:16
John 3:16 John 3:16 John 3:16 John 3:16
John 3:16 John 3:16 John 3:16 John 3:16
John 3:16 John 3:16 John 3:16 John 3:16
John 3:16 John 3:16 John 3:16 John 3:16
John 3:16 John 3:16 John 3:16 John 3:16
John 3:16 John 3:16 John 3:16 John 3:16
John 3:16 John 3:16 John 3:16 John 3:16
John 3:16 John 3:16 John 3:16 John 3:16
John 3:16 John 3:16 John 3:16 John 3:16
John 3:16 John 3:16 John 3:16 John 3:16
John 3:16 John 3:16 John 3:16 John 3:16
John 3:16 John 3:16 John 3:16 John 3:16
John 3:16 John 3:16 John 3:16 John 3:16
John 3:16 John 3:16 John 3:16 John 3:16
John 3:16 John 3:16 John 3:16 John 3:16
John 3:16 John 3:16 John 3:16 John 3:16
John 3:16 John 3:16 John 3:16 John 3:16
John 3:16 John 3:16 John 3:16 John 3:16
John 3:16 John 3:16 John 3:16 John 3:16
John 3:16 John 3:16 John 3:16 John 3:16
John 3:16 John 3:16 John 3:16 John 3:16
John 3:16 John 3:16 John 3:16 John 3:16
John 3:16 John 3:16 John 3:16 John 3:16
John 3:16 John 3:16 John 3:16 John 3:16
John 3:16 John 3:16 John 3:16 John 3:16
John 3:16 John 3:16 John 3:16 John 3:16
John 3:16 John 3:16 John 3:16 John 3:16

John 3:16	John 3:16	John 3:16	John 3:16
John 3:16	John 3:16	John 3:16	John 3:16
John 3:16	John 3:16	John 3:16	John 3:16
John 3:16	John 3:16	John 3:16	John 3:16
John 3:16	John 3:16	John 3:16	John 3:16
John 3:16	John 3:16	John 3:16	John 3:16
John 3:16	John 3:16	John 3:16	John 3:16
John 3:16	John 3:16	John 3:16	John 3:16
John 3:16	John 3:16	John 3:16	John 3:16
John 3:16	John 3:16	John 3:16	John 3:16
John 3:16	John 3:16	John 3:16	John 3:16
John 3:16	John 3:16	John 3:16	John 3:16
John 3:16	John 3:16	John 3:16	John 3:16
John 3:16	John 3:16	John 3:16	John 3:16
John 3:16	John 3:16	John 3:16	John 3:16
John 3:16	John 3:16	John 3:16	John 3:16
John 3:16	John 3:16	John 3:16	John 3:16
John 3:16	John 3:16	John 3:16	John 3:16
John 3:16	John 3:16	John 3:16	John 3:16
John 3:16	John 3:16	John 3:16	John 3:16
John 3:16	John 3:16	John 3:16	John 3:16
John 3:16	John 3:16	John 3:16	John 3:16
John 3:16	John 3:16	John 3:16	John 3:16

<u>But, God Is Love???</u>

John 3:16	John 3:16	John 3:16	John 3:16
John 3:16	John 3:16	John 3:16	John 3:16
John 3:16	John 3:16	John 3:16	John 3:16
John 3:16	John 3:16	John 3:16	John 3:16
John 3:16	John 3:16	John 3:16	John 3:16
John 3:16	John 3:16	John 3:16	John 3:16
John 3:16	John 3:16	John 3:16	John 3:16
John 3:16	John 3:16	John 3:16	John 3:16
John 3:16	John 3:16	John 3:16	John 3:16
John 3:16	John 3:16	John 3:16	John 3:16
John 3:16	John 3:16	John 3:16	John 3:16
John 3:16	John 3:16	John 3:16	John 3:16
John 3:16	John 3:16	John 3:16	John 3:16
John 3:16	John 3:16	John 3:16	John 3:16
John 3:16	John 3:16	John 3:16	John 3:16
John 3:16	John 3:16	John 3:16	John 3:16
John 3:16	John 3:16	John 3:16	John 3:16
John 3:16	John 3:16	John 3:16	John 3:16
John 3:16	John 3:16	John 3:16	John 3:16
John 3:16	John 3:16	John 3:16	John 3:16
John 3:16	John 3:16	John 3:16	John 3:16
John 3:16	John 3:16	John 3:16	John 3:16
John 3:16	John 3:16	John 3:16	John 3:16
John 3:16	John 3:16	John 3:16	John 3:16

John 3:16	John 3:16	John 3:16	John 3:16
John 3:16	John 3:16	John 3:16	John 3:16
John 3:16	John 3:16	John 3:16	John 3:16
John 3:16	John 3:16	John 3:16	John 3:16
John 3:16	John 3:16	John 3:16	John 3:16
John 3:16	John 3:16	John 3:16	John 3:16
John 3:16	John 3:16	John 3:16	John 3:16
John 3:16	John 3:16	John 3:16	John 3:16
John 3:16	John 3:16	John 3:16	John 3:16
John 3:16	John 3:16	John 3:16	John 3:16
John 3:16	John 3:16	John 3:16	John 3:16
John 3:16	John 3:16	John 3:16	John 3:16
John 3:16	John 3:16	John 3:16	John 3:16
John 3:16	John 3:16	John 3:16	John 3:16
John 3:16	John 3:16	John 3:16	John 3:16
John 3:16	John 3:16	John 3:16	John 3:16
John 3:16	John 3:16	John 3:16	John 3:16
John 3:16	John 3:16	John 3:16	John 3:16
John 3:16	John 3:16	John 3:16	John 3:16
John 3:16	John 3:16	John 3:16	John 3:16
John 3:16	John 3:16	John 3:16	John 3:16
John 3:16	John 3:16	John 3:16	John 3:16
John 3:16	John 3:16	John 3:16	John 3:16
John 3:16	John 3:16	John 3:16	John 3:16
John 3:16	John 3:16	John 3:16	John 3:16
John 3:16	John 3:16	John 3:16	John 3:16

John 3:16	John 3:16	John 3:16	John 3:16
John 3:16	John 3:16	John 3:16	John 3:16
John 3:16	John 3:16	John 3:16	John 3:16
John 3:16	John 3:16	John 3:16	John 3:16
John 3:16	John 3:16	John 3:16	John 3:16
John 3:16	John 3:16	John 3:16	John 3:16
John 3:16	John 3:16	John 3:16	John 3:16
John 3:16	John 3:16	John 3:16	John 3:16
John 3:16	John 3:16	John 3:16	John 3:16
John 3:16	John 3:16	John 3:16	John 3:16
John 3:16	John 3:16	John 3:16	John 3:16
John 3:16	John 3:16	John 3:16	John 3:16
John 3:16	John 3:16	John 3:16	John 3:16
John 3:16	John 3:16	John 3:16	John 3:16
John 3:16	John 3:16	John 3:16	John 3:16
John 3:16	John 3:16	John 3:16	John 3:16
John 3:16	John 3:16	John 3:16	John 3:16
John 3:16	John 3:16	John 3:16	John 3:16
John 3:16	John 3:16	John 3:16	John 3:16
John 3:16	John 3:16	John 3:16	John 3:16
John 3:16	John 3:16	John 3:16	John 3:16
John 3:16	John 3:16	John 3:16	John 3:16
John 3:16	John 3:16	John 3:16	John 3:16
John 3:16	John 3:16	John 3:16	John 3:16

John 3:16	John 3:16	John 3:16	John 3:16
John 3:16	John 3:16	John 3:16	John 3:16
John 3:16	John 3:16	John 3:16	John 3:16
John 3:16	John 3:16	John 3:16	John 3:16
John 3:16	John 3:16	John 3:16	John 3:16
John 3:16	John 3:16	John 3:16	John 3:16
John 3:16	John 3:16	John 3:16	John 3:16
John 3:16	John 3:16	John 3:16	John 3:16
John 3:16	John 3:16	John 3:16	John 3:16
John 3:16	John 3:16	John 3:16	John 3:16
John 3:16	John 3:16	John 3:16	John 3:16
John 3:16	John 3:16	John 3:16	John 3:16
John 3:16	John 3:16	John 3:16	John 3:16
John 3:16	John 3:16	John 3:16	John 3:16
John 3:16	John 3:16	John 3:16	John 3:16
John 3:16	John 3:16	John 3:16	John 3:16
John 3:16	John 3:16	John 3:16	John 3:16
John 3:16	John 3:16	John 3:16	John 3:16
John 3:16	John 3:16	John 3:16	John 3:16
John 3:16	John 3:16	John 3:16	John 3:16
John 3:16	John 3:16	John 3:16	John 3:16
John 3:16	John 3:16	John 3:16	John 3:16
John 3:16	John 3:16	John 3:16	John 3:16
John 3:16	John 3:16	John 3:16	John 3:16
John 3:16	John 3:16	John 3:16	John 3:16
John 3:16	John 3:16	John 3:16	John 3:16

John 3:16	John 3:16	John 3:16	John 3:16
John 3:16	John 3:16	John 3:16	John 3:16
John 3:16	John 3:16	John 3:16	John 3:16
John 3:16	John 3:16	John 3:16	John 3:16
John 3:16	John 3:16	John 3:16	John 3:16
John 3:16	John 3:16	John 3:16	John 3:16
John 3:16	John 3:16	John 3:16	John 3:16
John 3:16	John 3:16	John 3:16	John 3:16
John 3:16	John 3:16	John 3:16	John 3:16
John 3:16	John 3:16	John 3:16	John 3:16
John 3:16	John 3:16	John 3:16	John 3:16
John 3:16	John 3:16	John 3:16	John 3:16
John 3:16	John 3:16	John 3:16	John 3:16
John 3:16	John 3:16	John 3:16	John 3:16
John 3:16	John 3:16	John 3:16	John 3:16
John 3:16	John 3:16	John 3:16	John 3:16
John 3:16	John 3:16	John 3:16	John 3:16
John 3:16	John 3:16	John 3:16	John 3:16
John 3:16	John 3:16	John 3:16	John 3:16
John 3:16	John 3:16	John 3:16	John 3:16
John 3:16	John 3:16	John 3:16	John 3:16
John 3:16	John 3:16	John 3:16	John 3:16
John 3:16	John 3:16	John 3:16	John 3:16
John 3:16	John 3:16	John 3:16	John 3:16
John 3:16	John 3:16	John 3:16	John 3:16

John 3:16   John 3:16   John 3:16   John 3:16
John 3:16   John 3:16   John 3:16   John 3:16
John 3:16   John 3:16   John 3:16   John 3:16
John 3:16   John 3:16   John 3:16   John 3:16
John 3:16   John 3:16   John 3:16   John 3:16
John 3:16   John 3:16   John 3:16   John 3:16
John 3:16   John 3:16   John 3:16   John 3:16
John 3:16   John 3:16   John 3:16   John 3:16
John 3:16   John 3:16   John 3:16   John 3:16
John 3:16   John 3:16   John 3:16   John 3:16
John 3:16   John 3:16   John 3:16   John 3:16
John 3:16   John 3:16   John 3:16   John 3:16
John 3:16   John 3:16   John 3:16   John 3:16
John 3:16   John 3:16   John 3:16   John 3:16
John 3:16   John 3:16   John 3:16   John 3:16
John 3:16   John 3:16   John 3:16   John 3:16
John 3:16   John 3:16   John 3:16   John 3:16
John 3:16   John 3:16   John 3:16   John 3:16
John 3:16   John 3:16   John 3:16   John 3:16
John 3:16   John 3:16   John 3:16   John 3:16
John 3:16   John 3:16   John 3:16   John 3:16
John 3:16   John 3:16   John 3:16   John 3:16
John 3:16   John 3:16   John 3:16   John 3:16
John 3:16   John 3:16   John 3:16   John 3:16

His Love Tho???

I John 4:8b;	I John 4:8b;	I John 4:8b
I John 4:8b;	I John 4:8b;	I John 4:8b
I John 4:8b;	I John 4:8b;	I John 4:8b
I John 4:8b;	I John 4:8b;	I John 4:8b
I John 4:8b;	I John 4:8b;	I John 4:8b
I John 4:8b;	I John 4:8b;	I John 4:8b
I John 4:8b;	I John 4:8b;	I John 4:8b
I John 4:8b;	I John 4:8b;	I John 4:8b
I John 4:8b;	I John 4:8b;	I John 4:8b
I John 4:8b;	I John 4:8b;	I John 4:8b
I John 4:8b;	I John 4:8b;	I John 4:8b
I John 4:8b;	I John 4:8b;	I John 4:8b
I John 4:8b;	I John 4:8b;	I John 4:8b
I John 4:8b;	I John 4:8b;	I John 4:8b
I John 4:8b;	I John 4:8b;	I John 4:8b
I John 4:8b;	I John 4:8b;	I John 4:8b
I John 4:8b;	I John 4:8b;	I John 4:8b
I John 4:8b;	I John 4:8b;	I John 4:8b
I John 4:8b;	I John 4:8b;	I John 4:8b
I John 4:8b;	I John 4:8b;	I John 4:8b
I John 4:8b;	I John 4:8b;	I John 4:8b
I John 4:8b;	I John 4:8b;	I John 4:8b
I John 4:8b;	I John 4:8b;	I John 4:8b

I John 4:8b;   I John 4:8b;   I John 4:8b

I John 4:8b;   I John 4:8b;   I John 4:8b

I John 4:8b;   I John 4:8b;   I John 4:8b

I John 4:8b;   I John 4:8b;   I John 4:8b

I John 4:8b;   I John 4:8b;   I John 4:8b

I John 4:8b;   I John 4:8b;   I John 4:8b

I John 4:8b;   I John 4:8b;   I John 4:8b

I John 4:8b;   I John 4:8b;   I John 4:8b

I John 4:8b;   I John 4:8b;   I John 4:8b

I John 4:8b;   I John 4:8b;   I John 4:8b

I John 4:8b;   I John 4:8b;   I John 4:8b

I John 4:8b;   I John 4:8b;   I John 4:8b

I John 4:8b;   I John 4:8b;   I John 4:8b

I John 4:8b;   I John 4:8b;   I John 4:8b

I John 4:8b;   I John 4:8b;   I John 4:8b

I John 4:8b;   I John 4:8b;   I John 4:8b

I John 4:8b;   I John 4:8b;   I John 4:8b

I John 4:8b;   I John 4:8b;   I John 4:8b

I John 4:8b;   I John 4:8b;   I John 4:8b

I John 4:8b;   I John 4:8b;   I John 4:8b

I John 4:8b;   I John 4:8b;   I John 4:8b

I John 4:8b;   I John 4:8b;   I John 4:8b

I John 4:8b;   I John 4:8b;   I John 4:8b

I John 4:8b;   I John 4:8b;   I John 4:8b

I John 4:8b;   I John 4:8b;   I John 4:8b

I John 4:8b;   I John 4:8b;   I John 4:8b

I John 4:8b;   I John 4:8b;   I John 4:8b

I John 4:8b;   I John 4:8b;   I John 4:8b

I John 4:8b;   I John 4:8b;   I John 4:8b

I John 4:8b; I John 4:8b; I John 4:8b
I John 4:8b; I John 4:8b; I John 4:8b
I John 4:8b; I John 4:8b; I John 4:8b
I John 4:8b; I John 4:8b; I John 4:8b
I John 4:8b; I John 4:8b; I John 4:8b
I John 4:8b; I John 4:8b; I John 4:8b
I John 4:8b; I John 4:8b; I John 4:8b
I John 4:8b; I John 4:8b; I John 4:8b
I John 4:8b; I John 4:8b; I John 4:8b
I John 4:8b; I John 4:8b; I John 4:8b
I John 4:8b; I John 4:8b; I John 4:8b
I John 4:8b; I John 4:8b; I John 4:8b
I John 4:8b; I John 4:8b; I John 4:8b
I John 4:8b; I John 4:8b; I John 4:8b
I John 4:8b; I John 4:8b; I John 4:8b
I John 4:8b; I John 4:8b; I John 4:8b
I John 4:8b; I John 4:8b; I John 4:8b
I John 4:8b; I John 4:8b; I John 4:8b
I John 4:8b; I John 4:8b; I John 4:8b
I John 4:8b; I John 4:8b; I John 4:8b
I John 4:8b; I John 4:8b; I John 4:8b
I John 4:8b; I John 4:8b; I John 4:8b
I John 4:8b; I John 4:8b; I John 4:8b
I John 4:8b; I John 4:8b; I John 4:8b
I John 4:8b; I John 4:8b; I John 4:8b
I John 4:8b; I John 4:8b; I John 4:8b
I John 4:8b; I John 4:8b; I John 4:8b

I John 4:8b;	I John 4:8b;	I John 4:8b
I John 4:8b;	I John 4:8b;	I John 4:8b
I John 4:8b;	I John 4:8b;	I John 4:8b
I John 4:8b;	I John 4:8b;	I John 4:8b
I John 4:8b;	I John 4:8b;	I John 4:8b
I John 4:8b;	I John 4:8b;	I John 4:8b
I John 4:8b;	I John 4:8b;	I John 4:8b
I John 4:8b;	I John 4:8b;	I John 4:8b
I John 4:8b;	I John 4:8b;	I John 4:8b
I John 4:8b;	I John 4:8b;	I John 4:8b
I John 4:8b;	I John 4:8b;	I John 4:8b
I John 4:8b;	I John 4:8b;	I John 4:8b
I John 4:8b;	I John 4:8b;	I John 4:8b
I John 4:8b;	I John 4:8b;	I John 4:8b
I John 4:8b;	I John 4:8b;	I John 4:8b
I John 4:8b;	I John 4:8b;	I John 4:8b
I John 4:8b;	I John 4:8b;	I John 4:8b
I John 4:8b;	I John 4:8b;	I John 4:8b
I John 4:8b;	I John 4:8b;	I John 4:8b
I John 4:8b;	I John 4:8b;	I John 4:8b
I John 4:8b;	I John 4:8b;	I John 4:8b
I John 4:8b;	I John 4:8b;	I John 4:8b
I John 4:8b;	I John 4:8b;	I John 4:8b
I John 4:8b;	I John 4:8b;	I John 4:8b
I John 4:8b;	I John 4:8b;	I John 4:8b
I John 4:8b;	I John 4:8b;	I John 4:8b

I John 4:8b;	I John 4:8b;	I John 4:8b
I John 4:8b;	I John 4:8b;	I John 4:8b
I John 4:8b;	I John 4:8b;	I John 4:8b
I John 4:8b;	I John 4:8b;	I John 4:8b
I John 4:8b;	I John 4:8b;	I John 4:8b
I John 4:8b;	I John 4:8b;	I John 4:8b
I John 4:8b;	I John 4:8b;	I John 4:8b
I John 4:8b;	I John 4:8b;	I John 4:8b
I John 4:8b;	I John 4:8b;	I John 4:8b
I John 4:8b;	I John 4:8b;	I John 4:8b
I John 4:8b;	I John 4:8b;	I John 4:8b
I John 4:8b;	I John 4:8b;	I John 4:8b
I John 4:8b;	I John 4:8b;	I John 4:8b
I John 4:8b;	I John 4:8b;	I John 4:8b
I John 4:8b;	I John 4:8b;	I John 4:8b
I John 4:8b;	I John 4:8b;	I John 4:8b
I John 4:8b;	I John 4:8b;	I John 4:8b
I John 4:8b;	I John 4:8b;	I John 4:8b
I John 4:8b;	I John 4:8b;	I John 4:8b
I John 4:8b;	I John 4:8b;	I John 4:8b
I John 4:8b;	I John 4:8b;	I John 4:8b
I John 4:8b;	I John 4:8b;	I John 4:8b
I John 4:8b;	I John 4:8b;	I John 4:8b
I John 4:8b;	I John 4:8b;	I John 4:8b
I John 4:8b;	I John 4:8b;	I John 4:8b
I John 4:8b;	I John 4:8b;	I John 4:8b

I John 4:8b;   I John 4:8b;   I John 4:8b
I John 4:8b;   I John 4:8b;   I John 4:8b
I John 4:8b;   I John 4:8b;   I John 4:8b
I John 4:8b;   I John 4:8b;   I John 4:8b
I John 4:8b;   I John 4:8b;   I John 4:8b
I John 4:8b;   I John 4:8b;   I John 4:8b
I John 4:8b;   I John 4:8b;   I John 4:8b
I John 4:8b;   I John 4:8b;   I John 4:8b
I John 4:8b;   I John 4:8b;   I John 4:8b
I John 4:8b;   I John 4:8b;   I John 4:8b
I John 4:8b;   I John 4:8b;   I John 4:8b
I John 4:8b;   I John 4:8b;   I John 4:8b
I John 4:8b;   I John 4:8b;   I John 4:8b
I John 4:8b;   I John 4:8b;   I John 4:8b
I John 4:8b;   I John 4:8b;   I John 4:8b
I John 4:8b;   I John 4:8b;   I John 4:8b
I John 4:8b;   I John 4:8b;   I John 4:8b
I John 4:8b;   I John 4:8b;   I John 4:8b
I John 4:8b;   I John 4:8b;   I John 4:8b
I John 4:8b;   I John 4:8b;   I John 4:8b
I John 4:8b;   I John 4:8b;   I John 4:8b
I John 4:8b;   I John 4:8b;   I John 4:8b
I John 4:8b;   I John 4:8b;   I John 4:8b
I John 4:8b;   I John 4:8b;   I John 4:8b
I John 4:8b;   I John 4:8b;   I John 4:8b
I John 4:8b;   I John 4:8b;   I John 4:8b
I John 4:8b;   I John 4:8b;   I John 4:8b

I John 4:8b;   I John 4:8b;   I John 4:8b
I John 4:8b;   I John 4:8b;   I John 4:8b
I John 4:8b;   I John 4:8b;   I John 4:8b
I John 4:8b;   I John 4:8b;   I John 4:8b
I John 4:8b;   I John 4:8b;   I John 4:8b
I John 4:8b;   I John 4:8b;   I John 4:8b
I John 4:8b;   I John 4:8b;   I John 4:8b
I John 4:8b;   I John 4:8b;   I John 4:8b
I John 4:8b;   I John 4:8b;   I John 4:8b
I John 4:8b;   I John 4:8b;   I John 4:8b
I John 4:8b;   I John 4:8b;   I John 4:8b
I John 4:8b;   I John 4:8b;   I John 4:8b
I John 4:8b;   I John 4:8b;   I John 4:8b
I John 4:8b;   I John 4:8b;   I John 4:8b
I John 4:8b;   I John 4:8b;   I John 4:8b
I John 4:8b;   I John 4:8b;   I John 4:8b
I John 4:8b;   I John 4:8b;   I John 4:8b
I John 4:8b;   I John 4:8b;   I John 4:8b
I John 4:8b;   I John 4:8b;   I John 4:8b
I John 4:8b;   I John 4:8b;   I John 4:8b
I John 4:8b;   I John 4:8b;   I John 4:8b
I John 4:8b;   I John 4:8b;   I John 4:8b
I John 4:8b;   I John 4:8b;   I John 4:8b
I John 4:8b;   I John 4:8b;   I John 4:8b
I John 4:8b;   I John 4:8b;   I John 4:8b
I John 4:8b;   I John 4:8b;   I John 4:8b
I John 4:8b;   I John 4:8b;   I John 4:8b

I John 4:8b;   I John 4:8b;   I John 4:8b
I John 4:8b;   I John 4:8b;   I John 4:8b
I John 4:8b;   I John 4:8b;   I John 4:8b
I John 4:8b;   I John 4:8b;   I John 4:8b
I John 4:8b;   I John 4:8b;   I John 4:8b
I John 4:8b;   I John 4:8b;   I John 4:8b
I John 4:8b;   I John 4:8b;   I John 4:8b
I John 4:8b;   I John 4:8b;   I John 4:8b
I John 4:8b;   I John 4:8b;   I John 4:8b
I John 4:8b;   I John 4:8b;   I John 4:8b
I John 4:8b;   I John 4:8b;   I John 4:8b
I John 4:8b;   I John 4:8b;   I John 4:8b
I John 4:8b;   I John 4:8b;   I John 4:8b
I John 4:8b;   I John 4:8b;   I John 4:8b
I John 4:8b;   I John 4:8b;   I John 4:8b
I John 4:8b;   I John 4:8b;   I John 4:8b
I John 4:8b;   I John 4:8b;   I John 4:8b
I John 4:8b;   I John 4:8b;   I John 4:8b
I John 4:8b;   I John 4:8b;   I John 4:8b
I John 4:8b;   I John 4:8b;   I John 4:8b
I John 4:8b;   I John 4:8b;   I John 4:8b
I John 4:8b;   I John 4:8b;   I John 4:8b
I John 4:8b;   I John 4:8b;   I John 4:8b
I John 4:8b;   I John 4:8b;   I John 4:8b
I John 4:8b;   I John 4:8b;   I John 4:8b
I John 4:8b;   I John 4:8b;   I John 4:8b
I John 4:8b;   I John 4:8b;   I John 4:8b
I John 4:8b;   I John 4:8b;   I John 4:8b

I John 4:8b;	I John 4:8b;	I John 4:8b
I John 4:8b;	I John 4:8b;	I John 4:8b
I John 4:8b;	I John 4:8b;	I John 4:8b
I John 4:8b;	I John 4:8b;	I John 4:8b
I John 4:8b;	I John 4:8b;	I John 4:8b
I John 4:8b;	I John 4:8b;	I John 4:8b
I John 4:8b;	I John 4:8b;	I John 4:8b
I John 4:8b;	I John 4:8b;	I John 4:8b
I John 4:8b;	I John 4:8b;	I John 4:8b
I John 4:8b;	I John 4:8b;	I John 4:8b
I John 4:8b;	I John 4:8b;	I John 4:8b
I John 4:8b;	I John 4:8b;	I John 4:8b
I John 4:8b;	I John 4:8b;	I John 4:8b
I John 4:8b;	I John 4:8b;	I John 4:8b
I John 4:8b;	I John 4:8b;	I John 4:8b
I John 4:8b;	I John 4:8b;	I John 4:8b
I John 4:8b;	I John 4:8b;	I John 4:8b
I John 4:8b;	I John 4:8b;	I John 4:8b
I John 4:8b;	I John 4:8b;	I John 4:8b
I John 4:8b;	I John 4:8b;	I John 4:8b
I John 4:8b;	I John 4:8b;	I John 4:8b
I John 4:8b;	I John 4:8b;	I John 4:8b
I John 4:8b;	I John 4:8b;	I John 4:8b

I John 4:8b;   I John 4:8b;   I John 4:8b
I John 4:8b;   I John 4:8b;   I John 4:8b
I John 4:8b;   I John 4:8b;   I John 4:8b
I John 4:8b;   I John 4:8b;   I John 4:8b
I John 4:8b;   I John 4:8b;   I John 4:8b
I John 4:8b;   I John 4:8b;   I John 4:8b
I John 4:8b;   I John 4:8b;   I John 4:8b
I John 4:8b;   I John 4:8b;   I John 4:8b
I John 4:8b;   I John 4:8b;   I John 4:8b
I John 4:8b;   I John 4:8b;   I John 4:8b
I John 4:8b;   I John 4:8b;   I John 4:8b
I John 4:8b;   I John 4:8b;   I John 4:8b
I John 4:8b;   I John 4:8b;   I John 4:8b
I John 4:8b;   I John 4:8b;   I John 4:8b
I John 4:8b;   I John 4:8b;   I John 4:8b
I John 4:8b;   I John 4:8b;   I John 4:8b
I John 4:8b;   I John 4:8b;   I John 4:8b
I John 4:8b;   I John 4:8b;   I John 4:8b
I John 4:8b;   I John 4:8b;   I John 4:8b
I John 4:8b;   I John 4:8b;   I John 4:8b
I John 4:8b;   I John 4:8b;   I John 4:8b
I John 4:8b;   I John 4:8b;   I John 4:8b
I John 4:8b;   I John 4:8b;   I John 4:8b
I John 4:8b;   I John 4:8b;   I John 4:8b
I John 4:8b;   I John 4:8b;   I John 4:8b

I John 4:8b;   I John 4:8b;   I John 4:8b
I John 4:8b;   I John 4:8b;   I John 4:8b
I John 4:8b;   I John 4:8b;   I John 4:8b
I John 4:8b;   I John 4:8b;   I John 4:8b
I John 4:8b;   I John 4:8b;   I John 4:8b
I John 4:8b;   I John 4:8b;   I John 4:8b
I John 4:8b;   I John 4:8b;   I John 4:8b
I John 4:8b;   I John 4:8b;   I John 4:8b
I John 4:8b;   I John 4:8b;   I John 4:8b
I John 4:8b;   I John 4:8b;   I John 4:8b
I John 4:8b;   I John 4:8b;   I John 4:8b
I John 4:8b;   I John 4:8b;   I John 4:8b
I John 4:8b;   I John 4:8b;   I John 4:8b
I John 4:8b;   I John 4:8b;   I John 4:8b
I John 4:8b;   I John 4:8b;   I John 4:8b
I John 4:8b;   I John 4:8b;   I John 4:8b
I John 4:8b;   I John 4:8b;   I John 4:8b
I John 4:8b;   I John 4:8b;   I John 4:8b
I John 4:8b;   I John 4:8b;   I John 4:8b
I John 4:8b;   I John 4:8b;   I John 4:8b
I John 4:8b;   I John 4:8b;   I John 4:8b
I John 4:8b;   I John 4:8b;   I John 4:8b
I John 4:8b;   I John 4:8b;   I John 4:8b
I John 4:8b;   I John 4:8b;   I John 4:8b
I John 4:8b;   I John 4:8b;   I John 4:8b
I John 4:8b;   I John 4:8b;   I John 4:8b

His Love Tho?

Love = Choice   Love = Choice   Love = Choice
Love = Choice   Love = Choice   Love = Choice
Love = Choice   Love = Choice   Love = Choice
Love = Choice   Love = Choice   Love = Choice
Love = Choice   Love = Choice   Love = Choice
Love = Choice   Love = Choice   Love = Choice
Love = Choice   Love = Choice   Love = Choice
Love = Choice   Love = Choice   Love = Choice
Love = Choice   Love = Choice   Love = Choice
Love = Choice   Love = Choice   Love = Choice
Love = Choice   Love = Choice   Love = Choice
Love = Choice   Love = Choice   Love = Choice
Love = Choice   Love = Choice   Love = Choice
Love = Choice   Love = Choice   Love = Choice
Love = Choice   Love = Choice   Love = Choice
Love = Choice   Love = Choice   Love = Choice
Love = Choice   Love = Choice   Love = Choice
Love = Choice   Love = Choice   Love = Choice
Love = Choice   Love = Choice   Love = Choice
Love = Choice   Love = Choice   Love = Choice
Love = Choice   Love = Choice   Love = Choice
Love = Choice   Love = Choice   Love = Choice
Love = Choice   Love = Choice   Love = Choice
Love = Choice   Love = Choice   Love = Choice
Love = Choice   Love = Choice   Love = Choice
Love = Choice   Love = Choice   Love = Choice
Love = Choice   Love = Choice

Love = Choice   Love = Choice   Love = Choice
Love = Choice   Love = Choice   Love = Choice
Love = Choice   Love = Choice   Love = Choice
Love = Choice   Love = Choice   Love = Choice
Love = Choice   Love = Choice   Love = Choice
Love = Choice   Love = Choice   Love = Choice
Love = Choice   Love = Choice   Love = Choice
Love = Choice   Love = Choice   Love = Choice
Love = Choice   Love = Choice   Love = Choice
Love = Choice   Love = Choice   Love = Choice
Love = Choice   Love = Choice   Love = Choice
Love = Choice   Love = Choice   Love = Choice
Love = Choice   Love = Choice   Love = Choice
Love = Choice   Love = Choice   Love = Choice
Love = Choice   Love = Choice   Love = Choice
Love = Choice   Love = Choice   Love = Choice
Love = Choice   Love = Choice   Love = Choice
Love = Choice   Love = Choice   Love = Choice
Love = Choice   Love = Choice   Love = Choice
Love = Choice   Love = Choice   Love = Choice
Love = Choice   Love = Choice   Love = Choice
Love = Choice   Love = Choice   Love = Choice
Love = Choice   Love = Choice   Love = Choice
Love = Choice   Love = Choice   Love = Choice
Love = Choice   Love = Choice   Love = Choice
Love = Choice   Love = Choice   Love = Choice

Love = Choice	Love = Choice	Love = Choice
Love = Choice	Love = Choice	Love = Choice
Love = Choice	Love = Choice	Love = Choice
Love = Choice	Love = Choice	Love = Choice
Love = Choice	Love = Choice	Love = Choice
Love = Choice	Love = Choice	Love = Choice
Love = Choice	Love = Choice	Love = Choice
Love = Choice	Love = Choice	Love = Choice
Love = Choice	Love = Choice	Love = Choice
Love = Choice	Love = Choice	Love = Choice
Love = Choice	Love = Choice	Love = Choice
Love = Choice	Love = Choice	Love = Choice
Love = Choice	Love = Choice	Love = Choice
Love = Choice	Love = Choice	Love = Choice
Love = Choice	Love = Choice	Love = Choice
Love = Choice	Love = Choice	Love = Choice
Love = Choice	Love = Choice	Love = Choice
Love = Choice	Love = Choice	Love = Choice
Love = Choice	Love = Choice	Love = Choice
Love = Choice	Love = Choice	Love = Choice
Love = Choice	Love = Choice	Love = Choice
Love = Choice	Love = Choice	Love = Choice
Love = Choice	Love = Choice	Love = Choice
Love = Choice	Love = Choice	Love = Choice
Love = Choice	Love = Choice	Love = Choice
Love = Choice	Love = Choice	Love = Choice
Love = Choice	Love = Choice	Love = Choice
Love = Choice	Love = Choice	Love = Choice

Love = Choice	Love = Choice	Love = Choice
Love = Choice	Love = Choice	Love = Choice
Love = Choice	Love = Choice	Love = Choice
Love = Choice	Love = Choice	Love = Choice
Love = Choice	Love = Choice	Love = Choice
Love = Choice	Love = Choice	Love = Choice
Love = Choice	Love = Choice	Love = Choice
Love = Choice	Love = Choice	Love = Choice
Love = Choice	Love = Choice	Love = Choice
Love = Choice	Love = Choice	Love = Choice
Love = Choice	Love = Choice	Love = Choice
Love = Choice	Love = Choice	Love = Choice
Love = Choice	Love = Choice	Love = Choice
Love = Choice	Love = Choice	Love = Choice
Love = Choice	Love = Choice	Love = Choice
Love = Choice	Love = Choice	Love = Choice
Love = Choice	Love = Choice	Love = Choice
Love = Choice	Love = Choice	Love = Choice
Love = Choice	Love = Choice	Love = Choice
Love = Choice	Love = Choice	Love = Choice
Love = Choice	Love = Choice	Love = Choice
Love = Choice	Love = Choice	Love = Choice
Love = Choice	Love = Choice	Love = Choice
Love = Choice	Love = Choice	Love = Choice
Love = Choice	Love = Choice	Love = Choice
Love = Choice	Love = Choice	Love = Choice
Love = Choice	Love = Choice	Love = Choice
Love = Choice	Love = Choice	Love = Choice

Love = Choice   Love = Choice   Love = Choice
Love = Choice   Love = Choice   Love = Choice
Love = Choice   Love = Choice   Love = Choice
Love = Choice   Love = Choice   Love = Choice
Love = Choice   Love = Choice   Love = Choice
Love = Choice   Love = Choice   Love = Choice
Love = Choice   Love = Choice   Love = Choice
Love = Choice   Love = Choice   Love = Choice
Love = Choice   Love = Choice   Love = Choice
Love = Choice   Love = Choice   Love = Choice
Love = Choice   Love = Choice   Love = Choice
Love = Choice   Love = Choice   Love = Choice
Love = Choice   Love = Choice   Love = Choice
Love = Choice   Love = Choice   Love = Choice
Love = Choice   Love = Choice   Love = Choice
Love = Choice   Love = Choice   Love = Choice
Love = Choice   Love = Choice   Love = Choice
Love = Choice   Love = Choice   Love = Choice
Love = Choice   Love = Choice   Love = Choice
Love = Choice   Love = Choice   Love = Choice
Love = Choice   Love = Choice   Love = Choice
Love = Choice   Love = Choice   Love = Choice
Love = Choice   Love = Choice   Love = Choice

Love = Choice	Love = Choice	Love = Choice
Love = Choice	Love = Choice	Love = Choice
Love = Choice	Love = Choice	Love = Choice
Love = Choice	Love = Choice	Love = Choice
Love = Choice	Love = Choice	Love = Choice
Love = Choice	Love = Choice	Love = Choice
Love = Choice	Love = Choice	Love = Choice
Love = Choice	Love = Choice	Love = Choice
Love = Choice	Love = Choice	Love = Choice
Love = Choice	Love = Choice	Love = Choice
Love = Choice	Love = Choice	Love = Choice
Love = Choice	Love = Choice	Love = Choice
Love = Choice	Love = Choice	Love = Choice
Love = Choice	Love = Choice	Love = Choice
Love = Choice	Love = Choice	Love = Choice
Love = Choice	Love = Choice	Love = Choice
Love = Choice	Love = Choice	Love = Choice
Love = Choice	Love = Choice	Love = Choice
Love = Choice	Love = Choice	Love = Choice
Love = Choice	Love = Choice	Love = Choice
Love = Choice	Love = Choice	Love = Choice
Love = Choice	Love = Choice	Love = Choice
Love = Choice	Love = Choice	Love = Choice
Love = Choice	Love = Choice	Love = Choice
Love = Choice	Love = Choice	Love = Choice
Love = Choice	Love = Choice	Love = Choice
Love = Choice	Love = Choice	Love = Choice
Love = Choice	Love = Choice	Love = Choice
Love = Choice	Love = Choice	Love = Choice

Love = Choice Love = Choice Love = Choice
Love = Choice Love = Choice Love = Choice
Love = Choice Love = Choice Love = Choice
Love = Choice Love = Choice Love = Choice
Love = Choice Love = Choice Love = Choice
Love = Choice Love = Choice Love = Choice
Love = Choice Love = Choice Love = Choice
Love = Choice Love = Choice Love = Choice
Love = Choice Love = Choice Love = Choice
Love = Choice Love = Choice Love = Choice
Love = Choice Love = Choice Love = Choice
Love = Choice Love = Choice Love = Choice
Love = Choice Love = Choice Love = Choice
Love = Choice Love = Choice Love = Choice
Love = Choice Love = Choice Love = Choice
Love = Choice Love = Choice Love = Choice
Love = Choice Love = Choice Love = Choice
Love = Choice Love = Choice Love = Choice
Love = Choice Love = Choice Love = Choice
Love = Choice Love = Choice Love = Choice
Love = Choice Love = Choice Love = Choice
Love = Choice Love = Choice Love = Choice
Love = Choice Love = Choice Love = Choice
Love = Choice Love = Choice Love = Choice
Love = Choice Love = Choice Love = Choice
Love = Choice Love = Choice Love = Choice
Love = Choice Love = Choice

Love = Choice	Love = Choice	Love = Choice
Love = Choice	Love = Choice	Love = Choice
Love = Choice	Love = Choice	Love = Choice
Love = Choice	Love = Choice	Love = Choice
Love = Choice	Love = Choice	Love = Choice
Love = Choice	Love = Choice	Love = Choice
Love = Choice	Love = Choice	Love = Choice
Love = Choice	Love = Choice	Love = Choice
Love = Choice	Love = Choice	Love = Choice
Love = Choice	Love = Choice	Love = Choice
Love = Choice	Love = Choice	Love = Choice
Love = Choice	Love = Choice	Love = Choice
Love = Choice	Love = Choice	Love = Choice
Love = Choice	Love = Choice	Love = Choice
Love = Choice	Love = Choice	Love = Choice
Love = Choice	Love = Choice	Love = Choice
Love = Choice	Love = Choice	Love = Choice
Love = Choice	Love = Choice	Love = Choice
Love = Choice	Love = Choice	Love = Choice
Love = Choice	Love = Choice	Love = Choice
Love = Choice	Love = Choice	Love = Choice
Love = Choice	Love = Choice	Love = Choice
Love = Choice	Love = Choice	Love = Choice
Love = Choice	Love = Choice	Love = Choice
Love = Choice	Love = Choice	Love = Choice
Love = Choice	Love = Choice	Love = Choice
Love = Choice	Love = Choice	Love = Choice
Love = Choice	Love = Choice	Love = Choice

Love = Choice	Love = Choice	Love = Choice
Love = Choice	Love = Choice	Love = Choice
Love = Choice	Love = Choice	Love = Choice
Love = Choice	Love = Choice	Love = Choice
Love = Choice	Love = Choice	Love = Choice
Love = Choice	Love = Choice	Love = Choice
Love = Choice	Love = Choice	Love = Choice
Love = Choice	Love = Choice	Love = Choice
Love = Choice	Love = Choice	Love = Choice
Love = Choice	Love = Choice	Love = Choice
Love = Choice	Love = Choice	Love = Choice
Love = Choice	Love = Choice	Love = Choice
Love = Choice	Love = Choice	Love = Choice
Love = Choice	Love = Choice	Love = Choice
Love = Choice	Love = Choice	Love = Choice
Love = Choice	Love = Choice	Love = Choice
Love = Choice	Love = Choice	Love = Choice
Love = Choice	Love = Choice	Love = Choice
Love = Choice	Love = Choice	Love = Choice
Love = Choice	Love = Choice	Love = Choice
Love = Choice	Love = Choice	Love = Choice
Love = Choice	Love = Choice	Love = Choice
Love = Choice	Love = Choice	Love = Choice
Love = Choice	Love = Choice	Love = Choice
Love = Choice	Love = Choice	Love = Choice
Love = Choice	Love = Choice	Love = Choice
Love = Choice	Love = Choice	Love = Choice
Love = Choice	Love = Choice	

Love = Choice	Love = Choice	Love = Choice
Love = Choice	Love = Choice	Love = Choice
Love = Choice	Love = Choice	Love = Choice
Love = Choice	Love = Choice	Love = Choice
Love = Choice	Love = Choice	Love = Choice
Love = Choice	Love = Choice	Love = Choice
Love = Choice	Love = Choice	Love = Choice
Love = Choice	Love = Choice	Love = Choice
Love = Choice	Love = Choice	Love = Choice
Love = Choice	Love = Choice	Love = Choice
Love = Choice	Love = Choice	Love = Choice
Love = Choice	Love = Choice	Love = Choice
Love = Choice	Love = Choice	Love = Choice
Love = Choice	Love = Choice	Love = Choice
Love = Choice	Love = Choice	Love = Choice
Love = Choice	Love = Choice	Love = Choice
Love = Choice	Love = Choice	Love = Choice
Love = Choice	Love = Choice	Love = Choice
Love = Choice	Love = Choice	Love = Choice
Love = Choice	Love = Choice	Love = Choice
Love = Choice	Love = Choice	Love = Choice
Love = Choice	Love = Choice	Love = Choice
Love = Choice	Love = Choice	Love = Choice
Love = Choice	Love = Choice	Love = Choice
Love = Choice	Love = Choice	Love = Choice
Love = Choice	Love = Choice	Love = Choice
Love = Choice	Love = Choice	Love = Choice

That's Not FAIR!!!

That's Not FAIR!!!
That's Not FAIR!!!
That's Not FAIR!!!
That's Not FAIR!!!
That's Not FAIR!!!
That's Not FAIR!!!
That's Not FAIR!!!
That's Not FAIR!!!
That's Not FAIR!!!
That's Not FAIR!!!
That's Not FAIR!!!
That's Not FAIR!!!
That's Not FAIR!!!
That's Not FAIR!!!
That's Not FAIR!!!
That's Not FAIR!!!
That's Not FAIR!!!
That's Not FAIR!!!
That's Not FAIR!!!
That's Not FAIR!!!
That's Not FAIR!!!
That's Not FAIR!!!
That's Not FAIR!!!

That's Not FAIR!!!
That's Not FAIR!!!
That's Not FAIR!!!
That's Not FAIR!!!
That's Not FAIR!!!
That's Not FAIR!!!
That's Not FAIR!!!
That's Not FAIR!!!
That's Not FAIR!!!
That's Not FAIR!!!
That's Not FAIR!!!
That's Not FAIR!!!
That's Not FAIR!!!
That's Not FAIR!!!
That's Not FAIR!!!
That's Not FAIR!!!
That's Not FAIR!!!
That's Not FAIR!!!
That's Not FAIR!!!
That's Not FAIR!!!
That's Not FAIR!!!
That's Not FAIR!!!
That's Not FAIR!!!

That's Not FAIR!!!   That's Not FAIR!!!
That's Not FAIR!!!   That's Not FAIR!!!
That's Not FAIR!!!   That's Not FAIR!!!
That's Not FAIR!!!   That's Not FAIR!!!
That's Not FAIR!!!   That's Not FAIR!!!
That's Not FAIR!!!   That's Not FAIR!!!
That's Not FAIR!!!   That's Not FAIR!!!
That's Not FAIR!!!   That's Not FAIR!!!
That's Not FAIR!!!   That's Not FAIR!!!
That's Not FAIR!!!   That's Not FAIR!!!
That's Not FAIR!!!   That's Not FAIR!!!
That's Not FAIR!!!   That's Not FAIR!!!
That's Not FAIR!!!   That's Not FAIR!!!
That's Not FAIR!!!   That's Not FAIR!!!
That's Not FAIR!!!   That's Not FAIR!!!
That's Not FAIR!!!   That's Not FAIR!!!
That's Not FAIR!!!   That's Not FAIR!!!
That's Not FAIR!!!   That's Not FAIR!!!
That's Not FAIR!!!   That's Not FAIR!!!
That's Not FAIR!!!   That's Not FAIR!!!
That's Not FAIR!!!   That's Not FAIR!!!
That's Not FAIR!!!   That's Not FAIR!!!
That's Not FAIR!!!   That's Not FAIR!!!
That's Not FAIR!!!   That's Not FAIR!!!
That's Not FAIR!!!   That's Not FAIR!!!
That's Not FAIR!!!

That's Not FAIR!!!   That's Not FAIR!!!
That's Not FAIR!!!   That's Not FAIR!!!
That's Not FAIR!!!   That's Not FAIR!!!
That's Not FAIR!!!   That's Not FAIR!!!
That's Not FAIR!!!   That's Not FAIR!!!
That's Not FAIR!!!   That's Not FAIR!!!
That's Not FAIR!!!   That's Not FAIR!!!
That's Not FAIR!!!   That's Not FAIR!!!
That's Not FAIR!!!   That's Not FAIR!!!
That's Not FAIR!!!   That's Not FAIR!!!
That's Not FAIR!!!   That's Not FAIR!!!
That's Not FAIR!!!   That's Not FAIR!!!
That's Not FAIR!!!   That's Not FAIR!!!
That's Not FAIR!!!   That's Not FAIR!!!
That's Not FAIR!!!   That's Not FAIR!!!
That's Not FAIR!!!   That's Not FAIR!!!
That's Not FAIR!!!   That's Not FAIR!!!
That's Not FAIR!!!   That's Not FAIR!!!
That's Not FAIR!!!   That's Not FAIR!!!
That's Not FAIR!!!   That's Not FAIR!!!
That's Not FAIR!!!   That's Not FAIR!!!
That's Not FAIR!!!   That's Not FAIR!!!
That's Not FAIR!!!   That's Not FAIR!!!
That's Not FAIR!!!   That's Not FAIR!!!
That's Not FAIR!!!   That's Not FAIR!!!
That's Not FAIR!!!   That's Not FAIR!!!
That's Not FAIR!!!   That's Not FAIR!!!
That's Not FAIR!!!   That's Not FAIR!!!

That's Not FAIR!!!   That's Not FAIR!!!
That's Not FAIR!!!   That's Not FAIR!!!
That's Not FAIR!!!   That's Not FAIR!!!
That's Not FAIR!!!   That's Not FAIR!!!
That's Not FAIR!!!   That's Not FAIR!!!
That's Not FAIR!!!   That's Not FAIR!!!
That's Not FAIR!!!   That's Not FAIR!!!
That's Not FAIR!!!   That's Not FAIR!!!
That's Not FAIR!!!   That's Not FAIR!!!
That's Not FAIR!!!   That's Not FAIR!!!
That's Not FAIR!!!   That's Not FAIR!!!
That's Not FAIR!!!   That's Not FAIR!!!
That's Not FAIR!!!   That's Not FAIR!!!
That's Not FAIR!!!   That's Not FAIR!!!
That's Not FAIR!!!   That's Not FAIR!!!
That's Not FAIR!!!   That's Not FAIR!!!
That's Not FAIR!!!   That's Not FAIR!!!
That's Not FAIR!!!   That's Not FAIR!!!
That's Not FAIR!!!   That's Not FAIR!!!
That's Not FAIR!!!   That's Not FAIR!!!
That's Not FAIR!!!   That's Not FAIR!!!
That's Not FAIR!!!   That's Not FAIR!!!
That's Not FAIR!!!   That's Not FAIR!!!
That's Not FAIR!!!   That's Not FAIR!!!
That's Not FAIR!!!   That's Not FAIR!!!
That's Not FAIR!!!   That's Not FAIR!!!
That's Not FAIR!!!   That's Not FAIR!!!
That's Not FAIR!!!   That's Not FAIR!!!

That's Not FAIR!!!   That's Not FAIR!!!
That's Not FAIR!!!   That's Not FAIR!!!
That's Not FAIR!!!   That's Not FAIR!!!
That's Not FAIR!!!   That's Not FAIR!!!
That's Not FAIR!!!   That's Not FAIR!!!
That's Not FAIR!!!   That's Not FAIR!!!
That's Not FAIR!!!   That's Not FAIR!!!
That's Not FAIR!!!   That's Not FAIR!!!
That's Not FAIR!!!   That's Not FAIR!!!
That's Not FAIR!!!   That's Not FAIR!!!
That's Not FAIR!!!   That's Not FAIR!!!
That's Not FAIR!!!   That's Not FAIR!!!
That's Not FAIR!!!   That's Not FAIR!!!
That's Not FAIR!!!   That's Not FAIR!!!
That's Not FAIR!!!   That's Not FAIR!!!
That's Not FAIR!!!   That's Not FAIR!!!
That's Not FAIR!!!   That's Not FAIR!!!
That's Not FAIR!!!   That's Not FAIR!!!
That's Not FAIR!!!   That's Not FAIR!!!
That's Not FAIR!!!   That's Not FAIR!!!
That's Not FAIR!!!   That's Not FAIR!!!
That's Not FAIR!!!   That's Not FAIR!!!
That's Not FAIR!!!   That's Not FAIR!!!
That's Not FAIR!!!   That's Not FAIR!!!
That's Not FAIR!!!   That's Not FAIR!!!
That's Not FAIR!!!   That's Not FAIR!!!
That's Not FAIR!!!   That's Not FAIR!!!
That's Not FAIR!!!   That's Not FAIR!!!

That's Not FAIR!!!   That's Not FAIR!!!
That's Not FAIR!!!   That's Not FAIR!!!
That's Not FAIR!!!   That's Not FAIR!!!
That's Not FAIR!!!   That's Not FAIR!!!
That's Not FAIR!!!   That's Not FAIR!!!
That's Not FAIR!!!   That's Not FAIR!!!
That's Not FAIR!!!   That's Not FAIR!!!
That's Not FAIR!!!   That's Not FAIR!!!
That's Not FAIR!!!   That's Not FAIR!!!
That's Not FAIR!!!   That's Not FAIR!!!
That's Not FAIR!!!   That's Not FAIR!!!
That's Not FAIR!!!   That's Not FAIR!!!
That's Not FAIR!!!   That's Not FAIR!!!
That's Not FAIR!!!   That's Not FAIR!!!
That's Not FAIR!!!   That's Not FAIR!!!
That's Not FAIR!!!   That's Not FAIR!!!
That's Not FAIR!!!   That's Not FAIR!!!
That's Not FAIR!!!   That's Not FAIR!!!
That's Not FAIR!!!   That's Not FAIR!!!
That's Not FAIR!!!   That's Not FAIR!!!
That's Not FAIR!!!   That's Not FAIR!!!
That's Not FAIR!!!   That's Not FAIR!!!
That's Not FAIR!!!   That's Not FAIR!!!
That's Not FAIR!!!   That's Not FAIR!!!
That's Not FAIR!!!   That's Not FAIR!!!
That's Not FAIR!!!

That's Not FAIR!!!   That's Not FAIR!!!
That's Not FAIR!!!   That's Not FAIR!!!
That's Not FAIR!!!   That's Not FAIR!!!
That's Not FAIR!!!   That's Not FAIR!!!
That's Not FAIR!!!   That's Not FAIR!!!
That's Not FAIR!!!   That's Not FAIR!!!
That's Not FAIR!!!   That's Not FAIR!!!
That's Not FAIR!!!   That's Not FAIR!!!
That's Not FAIR!!!   That's Not FAIR!!!
That's Not FAIR!!!   That's Not FAIR!!!
That's Not FAIR!!!   That's Not FAIR!!!
That's Not FAIR!!!   That's Not FAIR!!!
That's Not FAIR!!!   That's Not FAIR!!!
That's Not FAIR!!!   That's Not FAIR!!!
That's Not FAIR!!!   That's Not FAIR!!!
That's Not FAIR!!!   That's Not FAIR!!!
That's Not FAIR!!!   That's Not FAIR!!!
That's Not FAIR!!!   That's Not FAIR!!!
That's Not FAIR!!!   That's Not FAIR!!!
That's Not FAIR!!!   That's Not FAIR!!!
That's Not FAIR!!!   That's Not FAIR!!!
That's Not FAIR!!!   That's Not FAIR!!!
That's Not FAIR!!!   That's Not FAIR!!!
That's Not FAIR!!!   That's Not FAIR!!!
That's Not FAIR!!!   That's Not FAIR!!!
That's Not FAIR!!!   That's Not FAIR!!!
That's Not FAIR!!!   That's Not FAIR!!!

That's Not FAIR!!!   That's Not FAIR!!!
That's Not FAIR!!!   That's Not FAIR!!!
That's Not FAIR!!!   That's Not FAIR!!!
That's Not FAIR!!!   That's Not FAIR!!!
That's Not FAIR!!!   That's Not FAIR!!!
That's Not FAIR!!!   That's Not FAIR!!!
That's Not FAIR!!!   That's Not FAIR!!!
That's Not FAIR!!!   That's Not FAIR!!!
That's Not FAIR!!!   That's Not FAIR!!!
That's Not FAIR!!!   That's Not FAIR!!!
That's Not FAIR!!!   That's Not FAIR!!!
That's Not FAIR!!!   That's Not FAIR!!!
That's Not FAIR!!!   That's Not FAIR!!!
That's Not FAIR!!!   That's Not FAIR!!!
That's Not FAIR!!!   That's Not FAIR!!!
That's Not FAIR!!!   That's Not FAIR!!!
That's Not FAIR!!!   That's Not FAIR!!!
That's Not FAIR!!!   That's Not FAIR!!!
That's Not FAIR!!!   That's Not FAIR!!!
That's Not FAIR!!!   That's Not FAIR!!!
That's Not FAIR!!!   That's Not FAIR!!!
That's Not FAIR!!!   That's Not FAIR!!!
That's Not FAIR!!!   That's Not FAIR!!!
That's Not FAIR!!!   That's Not FAIR!!!
That's Not FAIR!!!   That's Not FAIR!!!
That's Not FAIR!!!

That's Not FAIR!!! That's Not FAIR!!!
That's Not FAIR!!! That's Not FAIR!!!
That's Not FAIR!!! That's Not FAIR!!!
That's Not FAIR!!! That's Not FAIR!!!
That's Not FAIR!!! That's Not FAIR!!!
That's Not FAIR!!! That's Not FAIR!!!
That's Not FAIR!!! That's Not FAIR!!!
That's Not FAIR!!! That's Not FAIR!!!
That's Not FAIR!!! That's Not FAIR!!!
That's Not FAIR!!! That's Not FAIR!!!
That's Not FAIR!!! That's Not FAIR!!!
That's Not FAIR!!! That's Not FAIR!!!
That's Not FAIR!!! That's Not FAIR!!!
That's Not FAIR!!! That's Not FAIR!!!
That's Not FAIR!!! That's Not FAIR!!!
That's Not FAIR!!! That's Not FAIR!!!
That's Not FAIR!!! That's Not FAIR!!!
That's Not FAIR!!! That's Not FAIR!!!
That's Not FAIR!!! That's Not FAIR!!!
That's Not FAIR!!! That's Not FAIR!!!
That's Not FAIR!!! That's Not FAIR!!!
That's Not FAIR!!! That's Not FAIR!!!
That's Not FAIR!!! That's Not FAIR!!!
That's Not FAIR!!! That's Not FAIR!!!
That's Not FAIR!!! That's Not FAIR!!!
That's Not FAIR!!! That's Not FAIR!!!
That's Not FAIR!!! That's Not FAIR!!!

That's Not FAIR!!! That's Not FAIR!!!
That's Not FAIR!!! That's Not FAIR!!!
That's Not FAIR!!! That's Not FAIR!!!
That's Not FAIR!!! That's Not FAIR!!!
That's Not FAIR!!! That's Not FAIR!!!
That's Not FAIR!!! That's Not FAIR!!!
That's Not FAIR!!! That's Not FAIR!!!
That's Not FAIR!!! That's Not FAIR!!!
That's Not FAIR!!! That's Not FAIR!!!
That's Not FAIR!!! That's Not FAIR!!!
That's Not FAIR!!! That's Not FAIR!!!
That's Not FAIR!!! That's Not FAIR!!!
That's Not FAIR!!! That's Not FAIR!!!
That's Not FAIR!!! That's Not FAIR!!!
That's Not FAIR!!! That's Not FAIR!!!
That's Not FAIR!!! That's Not FAIR!!!
That's Not FAIR!!! That's Not FAIR!!!
That's Not FAIR!!! That's Not FAIR!!!
That's Not FAIR!!! That's Not FAIR!!!
That's Not FAIR!!! That's Not FAIR!!!
That's Not FAIR!!! That's Not FAIR!!!
That's Not FAIR!!! That's Not FAIR!!!
That's Not FAIR!!! That's Not FAIR!!!
That's Not FAIR!!! That's Not FAIR!!!
That's Not FAIR!!! That's Not FAIR!!!
That's Not FAIR!!! That's Not FAIR!!!
That's Not FAIR!!! That's Not FAIR!!!
That's Not FAIR!!! That's Not FAIR!!!

But, What About John 3:16???

John 3:16x2	John 3:16x2	John 3:16x2
John 3:16x2	John 3:16x2	John 3:16x2
John 3:16x2	John 3:16x2	John 3:16x2
John 3:16x2	John 3:16x2	John 3:16x2
John 3:16x2	John 3:16x2	John 3:16x2
John 3:16x2	John 3:16x2	John 3:16x2
John 3:16x2	John 3:16x2	John 3:16x2
John 3:16x2	John 3:16x2	John 3:16x2
John 3:16x2	John 3:16x2	John 3:16x2
John 3:16x2	John 3:16x2	John 3:16x2
John 3:16x2	John 3:16x2	John 3:16x2
John 3:16x2	John 3:16x2	John 3:16x2
John 3:16x2	John 3:16x2	John 3:16x2
John 3:16x2	John 3:16x2	John 3:16x2
John 3:16x2	John 3:16x2	John 3:16x2
John 3:16x2	John 3:16x2	John 3:16x2
John 3:16x2	John 3:16x2	John 3:16x2
John 3:16x2	John 3:16x2	John 3:16x2
John 3:16x2	John 3:16x2	John 3:16x2
John 3:16x2	John 3:16x2	John 3:16x2
John 3:16x2	John 3:16x2	John 3:16x2
John 3:16x2	John 3:16x2	John 3:16x2
John 3:16x2	John 3:16x2	John 3:16x2
John 3:16x2	John 3:16x2	John 3:16x2
John 3:16x2	John 3:16x2	John 3:16x2
John 3:16x2	John 3:16x2	John 3:16x2

John 3:16x2	John 3:16x2	John 3:16x2
John 3:16x2	John 3:16x2	John 3:16x2
John 3:16x2	John 3:16x2	John 3:16x2
John 3:16x2	John 3:16x2	John 3:16x2
John 3:16x2	John 3:16x2	John 3:16x2
John 3:16x2	John 3:16x2	John 3:16x2
John 3:16x2	John 3:16x2	John 3:16x2
John 3:16x2	John 3:16x2	John 3:16x2
John 3:16x2	John 3:16x2	John 3:16x2
John 3:16x2	John 3:16x2	John 3:16x2
John 3:16x2	John 3:16x2	John 3:16x2
John 3:16x2	John 3:16x2	John 3:16x2
John 3:16x2	John 3:16x2	John 3:16x2
John 3:16x2	John 3:16x2	John 3:16x2
John 3:16x2	John 3:16x2	John 3:16x2
John 3:16x2	John 3:16x2	John 3:16x2
John 3:16x2	John 3:16x2	John 3:16x2
John 3:16x2	John 3:16x2	John 3:16x2
John 3:16x2	John 3:16x2	John 3:16x2
John 3:16x2	John 3:16x2	John 3:16x2
John 3:16x2	John 3:16x2	John 3:16x2
John 3:16x2	John 3:16x2	John 3:16x2
John 3:16x2	John 3:16x2	John 3:16x2
John 3:16x2	John 3:16x2	John 3:16x2
John 3:16x2	John 3:16x2	John 3:16x2
John 3:16x2	John 3:16x2	John 3:16x2

John 3:16x2	John 3:16x2	John 3:16x2
John 3:16x2	John 3:16x2	John 3:16x2
John 3:16x2	John 3:16x2	John 3:16x2
John 3:16x2	John 3:16x2	John 3:16x2
John 3:16x2	John 3:16x2	John 3:16x2
John 3:16x2	John 3:16x2	John 3:16x2
John 3:16x2	John 3:16x2	John 3:16x2
John 3:16x2	John 3:16x2	John 3:16x2
John 3:16x2	John 3:16x2	John 3:16x2
John 3:16x2	John 3:16x2	John 3:16x2
John 3:16x2	John 3:16x2	John 3:16x2
John 3:16x2	John 3:16x2	John 3:16x2
John 3:16x2	John 3:16x2	John 3:16x2
John 3:16x2	John 3:16x2	John 3:16x2
John 3:16x2	John 3:16x2	John 3:16x2
John 3:16x2	John 3:16x2	John 3:16x2
John 3:16x2	John 3:16x2	John 3:16x2
John 3:16x2	John 3:16x2	John 3:16x2
John 3:16x2	John 3:16x2	John 3:16x2
John 3:16x2	John 3:16x2	John 3:16x2
John 3:16x2	John 3:16x2	John 3:16x2
John 3:16x2	John 3:16x2	John 3:16x2
John 3:16x2	John 3:16x2	John 3:16x2
John 3:16x2	John 3:16x2	John 3:16x2

John 3:16x2   John 3:16x2   John 3:16x2
John 3:16x2   John 3:16x2   John 3:16x2
John 3:16x2   John 3:16x2   John 3:16x2
John 3:16x2   John 3:16x2   John 3:16x2
John 3:16x2   John 3:16x2   John 3:16x2
John 3:16x2   John 3:16x2   John 3:16x2
John 3:16x2   John 3:16x2   John 3:16x2
John 3:16x2   John 3:16x2   John 3:16x2
John 3:16x2   John 3:16x2   John 3:16x2
John 3:16x2   John 3:16x2   John 3:16x2
John 3:16x2   John 3:16x2   John 3:16x2
John 3:16x2   John 3:16x2   John 3:16x2
John 3:16x2   John 3:16x2   John 3:16x2
John 3:16x2   John 3:16x2   John 3:16x2
John 3:16x2   John 3:16x2   John 3:16x2
John 3:16x2   John 3:16x2   John 3:16x2
John 3:16x2   John 3:16x2   John 3:16x2
John 3:16x2   John 3:16x2   John 3:16x2
John 3:16x2   John 3:16x2   John 3:16x2
John 3:16x2   John 3:16x2   John 3:16x2
John 3:16x2   John 3:16x2   John 3:16x2
John 3:16x2   John 3:16x2   John 3:16x2
John 3:16x2   John 3:16x2   John 3:16x2
John 3:16x2   John 3:16x2   John 3:16x2
John 3:16x2   John 3:16x2   John 3:16x2
John 3:16x2   John 3:16x2   John 3:16x2
John 3:16x2   John 3:16x2   John 3:16x2
John 3:16x2   John 3:16x2   John 3:16x2

John 3:16x2   John 3:16x2   John 3:16x2
John 3:16x2   John 3:16x2   John 3:16x2
John 3:16x2   John 3:16x2   John 3:16x2
John 3:16x2   John 3:16x2   John 3:16x2
John 3:16x2   John 3:16x2   John 3:16x2
John 3:16x2   John 3:16x2   John 3:16x2
John 3:16x2   John 3:16x2   John 3:16x2
John 3:16x2   John 3:16x2   John 3:16x2
John 3:16x2   John 3:16x2   John 3:16x2
John 3:16x2   John 3:16x2   John 3:16x2
John 3:16x2   John 3:16x2   John 3:16x2
John 3:16x2   John 3:16x2   John 3:16x2
John 3:16x2   John 3:16x2   John 3:16x2
John 3:16x2   John 3:16x2   John 3:16x2
John 3:16x2   John 3:16x2   John 3:16x2
John 3:16x2   John 3:16x2   John 3:16x2
John 3:16x2   John 3:16x2   John 3:16x2
John 3:16x2   John 3:16x2   John 3:16x2
John 3:16x2   John 3:16x2   John 3:16x2
John 3:16x2   John 3:16x2   John 3:16x2
John 3:16x2   John 3:16x2   John 3:16x2
John 3:16x2   John 3:16x2   John 3:16x2
John 3:16x2   John 3:16x2   John 3:16x2

John 3:16x2   John 3:16x2   John 3:16x2
John 3:16x2   John 3:16x2   John 3:16x2
John 3:16x2   John 3:16x2   John 3:16x2
John 3:16x2   John 3:16x2   John 3:16x2
John 3:16x2   John 3:16x2   John 3:16x2
John 3:16x2   John 3:16x2   John 3:16x2
John 3:16x2   John 3:16x2   John 3:16x2
John 3:16x2   John 3:16x2   John 3:16x2
John 3:16x2   John 3:16x2   John 3:16x2
John 3:16x2   John 3:16x2   John 3:16x2
John 3:16x2   John 3:16x2   John 3:16x2
John 3:16x2   John 3:16x2   John 3:16x2
John 3:16x2   John 3:16x2   John 3:16x2
John 3:16x2   John 3:16x2   John 3:16x2
John 3:16x2   John 3:16x2   John 3:16x2
John 3:16x2   John 3:16x2   John 3:16x2
John 3:16x2   John 3:16x2   John 3:16x2
John 3:16x2   John 3:16x2   John 3:16x2
John 3:16x2   John 3:16x2   John 3:16x2
John 3:16x2   John 3:16x2   John 3:16x2
John 3:16x2   John 3:16x2   John 3:16x2
John 3:16x2   John 3:16x2   John 3:16x2
John 3:16x2   John 3:16x2   John 3:16x2
John 3:16x2   John 3:16x2   John 3:16x2
John 3:16x2   John 3:16x2   John 3:16x2
John 3:16x2   John 3:16x2   John 3:16x2
John 3:16x2   John 3:16x2   John 3:16x2
John 3:16x2   John 3:16x2   John 3:16x2

John 3:16x2   John 3:16x2   John 3:16x2
John 3:16x2   John 3:16x2   John 3:16x2
John 3:16x2   John 3:16x2   John 3:16x2
John 3:16x2   John 3:16x2   John 3:16x2
John 3:16x2   John 3:16x2   John 3:16x2
John 3:16x2   John 3:16x2   John 3:16x2
John 3:16x2   John 3:16x2   John 3:16x2
John 3:16x2   John 3:16x2   John 3:16x2
John 3:16x2   John 3:16x2   John 3:16x2
John 3:16x2   John 3:16x2   John 3:16x2
John 3:16x2   John 3:16x2   John 3:16x2
John 3:16x2   John 3:16x2   John 3:16x2
John 3:16x2   John 3:16x2   John 3:16x2
John 3:16x2   John 3:16x2   John 3:16x2
John 3:16x2   John 3:16x2   John 3:16x2
John 3:16x2   John 3:16x2   John 3:16x2
John 3:16x2   John 3:16x2   John 3:16x2
John 3:16x2   John 3:16x2   John 3:16x2
John 3:16x2   John 3:16x2   John 3:16x2
John 3:16x2   John 3:16x2   John 3:16x2
John 3:16x2   John 3:16x2   John 3:16x2
John 3:16x2   John 3:16x2   John 3:16x2
John 3:16x2   John 3:16x2   John 3:16x2
John 3:16x2   John 3:16x2   John 3:16x2
John 3:16x2   John 3:16x2   John 3:16x2
John 3:16x2   John 3:16x2   John 3:16x2
John 3:16x2   John 3:16x2   John 3:16x2

John 3:16x2	John 3:16x2	John 3:16x2
John 3:16x2	John 3:16x2	John 3:16x2
John 3:16x2	John 3:16x2	John 3:16x2
John 3:16x2	John 3:16x2	John 3:16x2
John 3:16x2	John 3:16x2	John 3:16x2
John 3:16x2	John 3:16x2	John 3:16x2
John 3:16x2	John 3:16x2	John 3:16x2
John 3:16x2	John 3:16x2	John 3:16x2
John 3:16x2	John 3:16x2	John 3:16x2
John 3:16x2	John 3:16x2	John 3:16x2
John 3:16x2	John 3:16x2	John 3:16x2
John 3:16x2	John 3:16x2	John 3:16x2
John 3:16x2	John 3:16x2	John 3:16x2
John 3:16x2	John 3:16x2	John 3:16x2
John 3:16x2	John 3:16x2	John 3:16x2
John 3:16x2	John 3:16x2	John 3:16x2
John 3:16x2	John 3:16x2	John 3:16x2
John 3:16x2	John 3:16x2	John 3:16x2
John 3:16x2	John 3:16x2	John 3:16x2
John 3:16x2	John 3:16x2	John 3:16x2
John 3:16x2	John 3:16x2	John 3:16x2
John 3:16x2	John 3:16x2	John 3:16x2
John 3:16x2	John 3:16x2	John 3:16x2
John 3:16x2	John 3:16x2	John 3:16x2
John 3:16x2	John 3:16x2	John 3:16x2
John 3:16x2	John 3:16x2	John 3:16x2

John 3:16x2   John 3:16x2   John 3:16x2
John 3:16x2   John 3:16x2   John 3:16x2
John 3:16x2   John 3:16x2   John 3:16x2
John 3:16x2   John 3:16x2   John 3:16x2
John 3:16x2   John 3:16x2   John 3:16x2
John 3:16x2   John 3:16x2   John 3:16x2
John 3:16x2   John 3:16x2   John 3:16x2
John 3:16x2   John 3:16x2   John 3:16x2
John 3:16x2   John 3:16x2   John 3:16x2
John 3:16x2   John 3:16x2   John 3:16x2
John 3:16x2   John 3:16x2   John 3:16x2
John 3:16x2   John 3:16x2   John 3:16x2
John 3:16x2   John 3:16x2   John 3:16x2
John 3:16x2   John 3:16x2   John 3:16x2
John 3:16x2   John 3:16x2   John 3:16x2
John 3:16x2   John 3:16x2   John 3:16x2
John 3:16x2   John 3:16x2   John 3:16x2
John 3:16x2   John 3:16x2   John 3:16x2
John 3:16x2   John 3:16x2   John 3:16x2
John 3:16x2   John 3:16x2   John 3:16x2
John 3:16x2   John 3:16x2   John 3:16x2
John 3:16x2   John 3:16x2   John 3:16x2
John 3:16x2   John 3:16x2   John 3:16x2
John 3:16x2   John 3:16x2   John 3:16x2

John 3:16x2 John 3:16x2 John 3:16x2
John 3:16x2 John 3:16x2 John 3:16x2
John 3:16x2 John 3:16x2 John 3:16x2
John 3:16x2 John 3:16x2 John 3:16x2
John 3:16x2 John 3:16x2 John 3:16x2
John 3:16x2 John 3:16x2 John 3:16x2
John 3:16x2 John 3:16x2 John 3:16x2
John 3:16x2 John 3:16x2 John 3:16x2
John 3:16x2 John 3:16x2 John 3:16x2
John 3:16x2 John 3:16x2 John 3:16x2
John 3:16x2 John 3:16x2 John 3:16x2
John 3:16x2 John 3:16x2 John 3:16x2
John 3:16x2 John 3:16x2 John 3:16x2
John 3:16x2 John 3:16x2 John 3:16x2
John 3:16x2 John 3:16x2 John 3:16x2
John 3:16x2 John 3:16x2 John 3:16x2
John 3:16x2 John 3:16x2 John 3:16x2
John 3:16x2 John 3:16x2 John 3:16x2
John 3:16x2 John 3:16x2 John 3:16x2
John 3:16x2 John 3:16x2 John 3:16x2
John 3:16x2 John 3:16x2 John 3:16x2
John 3:16x2 John 3:16x2 John 3:16x2
John 3:16x2 John 3:16x2 John 3:16x2
John 3:16x2 John 3:16x2 John 3:16x2
John 3:16x2 John 3:16x2 John 3:16x2
John 3:16x2 John 3:16x2 John 3:16x2
John 3:16x2 John 3:16x2 John 3:16x2
John 3:16x2 John 3:16x2 John 3:16x2
John 3:16x2 John 3:16x2 John 3:16x2
John 3:16x2 John 3:16x2 John 3:16x2
John 3:16x2 John 3:16x2 John 3:16x2

Love Isn't Forced

True Love Is Not Forced
True Love Is Not Forced
True Love Is Not Forced
True Love Is Not Forced
True Love Is Not Forced
True Love Is Not Forced
True Love Is Not Forced
True Love Is Not Forced
True Love Is Not Forced
True Love Is Not Forced
True Love Is Not Forced
True Love Is Not Forced
True Love Is Not Forced
True Love Is Not Forced
True Love Is Not Forced
True Love Is Not Forced
True Love Is Not Forced
True Love Is Not Forced
True Love Is Not Forced
True Love Is Not Forced
True Love Is Not Forced
True Love Is Not Forced
True Love Is Not Forced
True Love Is Not Forced
True Love Is Not Forced
True Love Is Not Forced
True Love Is Not Forced

True Love Is Not Forced
True Love Is Not Forced
True Love Is Not Forced
True Love Is Not Forced
True Love Is Not Forced
True Love Is Not Forced
True Love Is Not Forced
True Love Is Not Forced
True Love Is Not Forced
True Love Is Not Forced
True Love Is Not Forced
True Love Is Not Forced
True Love Is Not Forced
True Love Is Not Forced
True Love Is Not Forced
True Love Is Not Forced
True Love Is Not Forced
True Love Is Not Forced
True Love Is Not Forced
True Love Is Not Forced
True Love Is Not Forced
True Love Is Not Forced
True Love Is Not Forced
True Love Is Not Forced
True Love Is Not Forced
True Love Is Not Forced
True Love Is Not Forced

True Love Is Not Forced
True Love Is Not Forced
True Love Is Not Forced
True Love Is Not Forced
True Love Is Not Forced
True Love Is Not Forced
True Love Is Not Forced
True Love Is Not Forced
True Love Is Not Forced
True Love Is Not Forced
True Love Is Not Forced
True Love Is Not Forced
True Love Is Not Forced
True Love Is Not Forced
True Love Is Not Forced
True Love Is Not Forced
True Love Is Not Forced
True Love Is Not Forced
True Love Is Not Forced
True Love Is Not Forced
True Love Is Not Forced
True Love Is Not Forced
True Love Is Not Forced
True Love Is Not Forced
True Love Is Not Forced
True Love Is Not Forced
True Love Is Not Forced
True Love Is Not Forced

True Love Is Not Forced
True Love Is Not Forced
True Love Is Not Forced
True Love Is Not Forced
True Love Is Not Forced
True Love Is Not Forced
True Love Is Not Forced
True Love Is Not Forced
True Love Is Not Forced
True Love Is Not Forced
True Love Is Not Forced
True Love Is Not Forced
True Love Is Not Forced
True Love Is Not Forced
True Love Is Not Forced
True Love Is Not Forced
True Love Is Not Forced
True Love Is Not Forced
True Love Is Not Forced
True Love Is Not Forced
True Love Is Not Forced
True Love Is Not Forced
True Love Is Not Forced
True Love Is Not Forced
True Love Is Not Forced
True Love Is Not Forced
True Love Is Not Forced
True Love Is Not Forced

True Love Is Not Forced
True Love Is Not Forced
True Love Is Not Forced
True Love Is Not Forced
True Love Is Not Forced
True Love Is Not Forced
True Love Is Not Forced
True Love Is Not Forced
True Love Is Not Forced
True Love Is Not Forced
True Love Is Not Forced
True Love Is Not Forced
True Love Is Not Forced
True Love Is Not Forced
True Love Is Not Forced
True Love Is Not Forced
True Love Is Not Forced
True Love Is Not Forced
True Love Is Not Forced
True Love Is Not Forced
True Love Is Not Forced
True Love Is Not Forced
True Love Is Not Forced
True Love Is Not Forced
True Love Is Not Forced
True Love Is Not Forced
True Love Is Not Forced
True Love Is Not Forced

True Love Is Not Forced
True Love Is Not Forced
True Love Is Not Forced
True Love Is Not Forced
True Love Is Not Forced
True Love Is Not Forced
True Love Is Not Forced
True Love Is Not Forced
True Love Is Not Forced
True Love Is Not Forced
True Love Is Not Forced
True Love Is Not Forced
True Love Is Not Forced
True Love Is Not Forced
True Love Is Not Forced
True Love Is Not Forced
True Love Is Not Forced
True Love Is Not Forced
True Love Is Not Forced
True Love Is Not Forced
True Love Is Not Forced
True Love Is Not Forced
True Love Is Not Forced
True Love Is Not Forced
True Love Is Not Forced
True Love Is Not Forced
True Love Is Not Forced
True Love Is Not Forced

True Love Is Not Forced True Love Is Not Forced
True Love Is Not Forced True Love Is Not Forced
True Love Is Not Forced True Love Is Not Forced
True Love Is Not Forced True Love Is Not Forced
True Love Is Not Forced True Love Is Not Forced
True Love Is Not Forced True Love Is Not Forced
True Love Is Not Forced True Love Is Not Forced
True Love Is Not Forced True Love Is Not Forced
True Love Is Not Forced True Love Is Not Forced
True Love Is Not Forced True Love Is Not Forced
True Love Is Not Forced True Love Is Not Forced
True Love Is Not Forced True Love Is Not Forced
True Love Is Not Forced True Love Is Not Forced
True Love Is Not Forced True Love Is Not Forced
True Love Is Not Forced True Love Is Not Forced
True Love Is Not Forced True Love Is Not Forced
True Love Is Not Forced True Love Is Not Forced
True Love Is Not Forced True Love Is Not Forced
True Love Is Not Forced True Love Is Not Forced
True Love Is Not Forced True Love Is Not Forced
True Love Is Not Forced True Love Is Not Forced
True Love Is Not Forced True Love Is Not Forced
True Love Is Not Forced True Love Is Not Forced
True Love Is Not Forced True Love Is Not Forced
True Love Is Not Forced True Love Is Not Forced
True Love Is Not Forced True Love Is Not Forced
True Love Is Not Forced True Love Is Not Forced

True Love Is Not Forced
True Love Is Not Forced
True Love Is Not Forced
True Love Is Not Forced
True Love Is Not Forced
True Love Is Not Forced
True Love Is Not Forced
True Love Is Not Forced
True Love Is Not Forced
True Love Is Not Forced
True Love Is Not Forced
True Love Is Not Forced
True Love Is Not Forced
True Love Is Not Forced
True Love Is Not Forced
True Love Is Not Forced
True Love Is Not Forced
True Love Is Not Forced
True Love Is Not Forced
True Love Is Not Forced
True Love Is Not Forced
True Love Is Not Forced
True Love Is Not Forced
True Love Is Not Forced
True Love Is Not Forced
True Love Is Not Forced
True Love Is Not Forced
True Love Is Not Forced
True Love Is Not Forced

True Love Is Not Forced
True Love Is Not Forced
True Love Is Not Forced
True Love Is Not Forced
True Love Is Not Forced
True Love Is Not Forced
True Love Is Not Forced
True Love Is Not Forced
True Love Is Not Forced
True Love Is Not Forced
True Love Is Not Forced
True Love Is Not Forced
True Love Is Not Forced
True Love Is Not Forced
True Love Is Not Forced
True Love Is Not Forced
True Love Is Not Forced
True Love Is Not Forced
True Love Is Not Forced
True Love Is Not Forced
True Love Is Not Forced
True Love Is Not Forced
True Love Is Not Forced
True Love Is Not Forced
True Love Is Not Forced
True Love Is Not Forced
True Love Is Not Forced
True Love Is Not Forced

True Love Is Not Forced   True Love Is Not Forced
True Love Is Not Forced   True Love Is Not Forced
True Love Is Not Forced   True Love Is Not Forced
True Love Is Not Forced   True Love Is Not Forced
True Love Is Not Forced   True Love Is Not Forced
True Love Is Not Forced   True Love Is Not Forced
True Love Is Not Forced   True Love Is Not Forced
True Love Is Not Forced   True Love Is Not Forced
True Love Is Not Forced   True Love Is Not Forced
True Love Is Not Forced   True Love Is Not Forced
True Love Is Not Forced   True Love Is Not Forced
True Love Is Not Forced   True Love Is Not Forced
True Love Is Not Forced   True Love Is Not Forced
True Love Is Not Forced   True Love Is Not Forced
True Love Is Not Forced   True Love Is Not Forced
True Love Is Not Forced   True Love Is Not Forced
True Love Is Not Forced   True Love Is Not Forced
True Love Is Not Forced   True Love Is Not Forced
True Love Is Not Forced   True Love Is Not Forced
True Love Is Not Forced   True Love Is Not Forced
True Love Is Not Forced   True Love Is Not Forced
True Love Is Not Forced   True Love Is Not Forced
True Love Is Not Forced   True Love Is Not Forced
True Love Is Not Forced   True Love Is Not Forced
True Love Is Not Forced   True Love Is Not Forced
True Love Is Not Forced   True Love Is Not Forced
True Love Is Not Forced   True Love Is Not Forced
True Love Is Not Forced   True Love Is Not Forced
True Love Is Not Forced

True Love Is Not Forced
True Love Is Not Forced
True Love Is Not Forced
True Love Is Not Forced
True Love Is Not Forced
True Love Is Not Forced
True Love Is Not Forced
True Love Is Not Forced
True Love Is Not Forced
True Love Is Not Forced
True Love Is Not Forced
True Love Is Not Forced
True Love Is Not Forced
True Love Is Not Forced
True Love Is Not Forced
True Love Is Not Forced
True Love Is Not Forced
True Love Is Not Forced
True Love Is Not Forced
True Love Is Not Forced
True Love Is Not Forced
True Love Is Not Forced
True Love Is Not Forced
True Love Is Not Forced
True Love Is Not Forced
True Love Is Not Forced
True Love Is Not Forced
True Love Is Not Forced

True Love Is Not Forced
True Love Is Not Forced
True Love Is Not Forced
True Love Is Not Forced
True Love Is Not Forced
True Love Is Not Forced
True Love Is Not Forced
True Love Is Not Forced
True Love Is Not Forced
True Love Is Not Forced
True Love Is Not Forced
True Love Is Not Forced
True Love Is Not Forced
True Love Is Not Forced
True Love Is Not Forced
True Love Is Not Forced
True Love Is Not Forced
True Love Is Not Forced
True Love Is Not Forced
True Love Is Not Forced
True Love Is Not Forced
True Love Is Not Forced
True Love Is Not Forced
True Love Is Not Forced
True Love Is Not Forced
True Love Is Not Forced
True Love Is Not Forced
True Love Is Not Forced

True Love Is Not Forced
True Love Is Not Forced
True Love Is Not Forced
True Love Is Not Forced
True Love Is Not Forced
True Love Is Not Forced
True Love Is Not Forced
True Love Is Not Forced
True Love Is Not Forced
True Love Is Not Forced
True Love Is Not Forced
True Love Is Not Forced
True Love Is Not Forced
True Love Is Not Forced
True Love Is Not Forced
True Love Is Not Forced
True Love Is Not Forced
True Love Is Not Forced
True Love Is Not Forced
True Love Is Not Forced
True Love Is Not Forced
True Love Is Not Forced
True Love Is Not Forced
True Love Is Not Forced
True Love Is Not Forced
True Love Is Not Forced

True Love Is Not Forced
True Love Is Not Forced
True Love Is Not Forced
True Love Is Not Forced
True Love Is Not Forced
True Love Is Not Forced
True Love Is Not Forced
True Love Is Not Forced
True Love Is Not Forced
True Love Is Not Forced
True Love Is Not Forced
True Love Is Not Forced
True Love Is Not Forced
True Love Is Not Forced
True Love Is Not Forced
True Love Is Not Forced
True Love Is Not Forced
True Love Is Not Forced
True Love Is Not Forced
True Love Is Not Forced
True Love Is Not Forced
True Love Is Not Forced
True Love Is Not Forced
True Love Is Not Forced
True Love Is Not Forced
True Love Is Not Forced

True Love Is Not Forced
True Love Is Not Forced
True Love Is Not Forced
True Love Is Not Forced
True Love Is Not Forced
True Love Is Not Forced
True Love Is Not Forced
True Love Is Not Forced
True Love Is Not Forced
True Love Is Not Forced
True Love Is Not Forced
True Love Is Not Forced
True Love Is Not Forced
True Love Is Not Forced
True Love Is Not Forced
True Love Is Not Forced
True Love Is Not Forced
True Love Is Not Forced
True Love Is Not Forced
True Love Is Not Forced
True Love Is Not Forced
True Love Is Not Forced
True Love Is Not Forced
True Love Is Not Forced
True Love Is Not Forced
True Love Is Not Forced
True Love Is Not Forced
True Love Is Not Forced

True Love Is Not Forced
True Love Is Not Forced
True Love Is Not Forced
True Love Is Not Forced
True Love Is Not Forced
True Love Is Not Forced
True Love Is Not Forced
True Love Is Not Forced
True Love Is Not Forced
True Love Is Not Forced
True Love Is Not Forced
True Love Is Not Forced
True Love Is Not Forced
True Love Is Not Forced
True Love Is Not Forced
True Love Is Not Forced
True Love Is Not Forced
True Love Is Not Forced
True Love Is Not Forced
True Love Is Not Forced
True Love Is Not Forced
True Love Is Not Forced
True Love Is Not Forced
True Love Is Not Forced
True Love Is Not Forced
True Love Is Not Forced
True Love Is Not Forced
True Love Is Not Forced

True Love Is Not Forced   True Love Is Not Forced
True Love Is Not Forced   True Love Is Not Forced
True Love Is Not Forced   True Love Is Not Forced
True Love Is Not Forced   True Love Is Not Forced
True Love Is Not Forced   True Love Is Not Forced
True Love Is Not Forced   True Love Is Not Forced
True Love Is Not Forced   True Love Is Not Forced
True Love Is Not Forced   True Love Is Not Forced
True Love Is Not Forced   True Love Is Not Forced
True Love Is Not Forced   True Love Is Not Forced
True Love Is Not Forced   True Love Is Not Forced
True Love Is Not Forced   True Love Is Not Forced
True Love Is Not Forced   True Love Is Not Forced
True Love Is Not Forced   True Love Is Not Forced
True Love Is Not Forced   True Love Is Not Forced
True Love Is Not Forced   True Love Is Not Forced
True Love Is Not Forced   True Love Is Not Forced
True Love Is Not Forced   True Love Is Not Forced
True Love Is Not Forced   True Love Is Not Forced
True Love Is Not Forced   True Love Is Not Forced
True Love Is Not Forced   True Love Is Not Forced
True Love Is Not Forced   True Love Is Not Forced
True Love Is Not Forced   True Love Is Not Forced
True Love Is Not Forced   True Love Is Not Forced
True Love Is Not Forced   True Love Is Not Forced
True Love Is Not Forced   True Love Is Not Forced
True Love Is Not Forced   True Love Is Not Forced
True Love Is Not Forced   True Love Is Not Forced
True Love Is Not Forced   True Love Is Not Forced

Didn't Calvin Kill Servetus???

Servetus! Servetus! Servetus! Servetus! Servetus
Servetus! Servetus! Servetus! Servetus! Servetus
Servetus! Servetus! Servetus! Servetus! Servetus
Servetus! Servetus! Servetus! Servetus! Servetus
Servetus! Servetus! Servetus! Servetus! Servetus
Servetus! Servetus! Servetus! Servetus! Servetus
Servetus! Servetus! Servetus! Servetus! Servetus
Servetus! Servetus! Servetus! Servetus! Servetus
Servetus! Servetus! Servetus! Servetus! Servetus
Servetus! Servetus! Servetus! Servetus! Servetus
Servetus! Servetus! Servetus! Servetus! Servetus
Servetus! Servetus! Servetus! Servetus! Servetus
Servetus! Servetus! Servetus! Servetus! Servetus
Servetus! Servetus! Servetus! Servetus! Servetus
Servetus! Servetus! Servetus! Servetus! Servetus
Servetus! Servetus! Servetus! Servetus! Servetus
Servetus! Servetus! Servetus! Servetus! Servetus
Servetus! Servetus! Servetus! Servetus! Servetus
Servetus! Servetus! Servetus! Servetus! Servetus
Servetus! Servetus! Servetus! Servetus! Servetus
Servetus! Servetus! Servetus! Servetus! Servetus
Servetus! Servetus! Servetus! Servetus! Servetus
Servetus! Servetus! Servetus! Servetus! Servetus
Servetus! Servetus! Servetus! Servetus! Servetus
Servetus! Servetus! Servetus! Servetus! Servetus
Servetus! Servetus! Servetus! Servetus! Servetus

Servetus! Servetus! Servetus! Servetus! Servetus
Servetus! Servetus! Servetus! Servetus! Servetus
Servetus! Servetus! Servetus! Servetus! Servetus
Servetus! Servetus! Servetus! Servetus! Servetus
Servetus! Servetus! Servetus! Servetus! Servetus
Servetus! Servetus! Servetus! Servetus! Servetus
Servetus! Servetus! Servetus! Servetus! Servetus
Servetus! Servetus! Servetus! Servetus! Servetus
Servetus! Servetus! Servetus! Servetus! Servetus
Servetus! Servetus! Servetus! Servetus! Servetus
Servetus! Servetus! Servetus! Servetus! Servetus
Servetus! Servetus! Servetus! Servetus! Servetus
Servetus! Servetus! Servetus! Servetus! Servetus
Servetus! Servetus! Servetus! Servetus! Servetus
Servetus! Servetus! Servetus! Servetus! Servetus
Servetus! Servetus! Servetus! Servetus! Servetus
Servetus! Servetus! Servetus! Servetus! Servetus
Servetus! Servetus! Servetus! Servetus! Servetus
Servetus! Servetus! Servetus! Servetus! Servetus
Servetus! Servetus! Servetus! Servetus! Servetus
Servetus! Servetus! Servetus! Servetus! Servetus
Servetus! Servetus! Servetus! Servetus! Servetus
Servetus! Servetus! Servetus! Servetus! Servetus
Servetus! Servetus! Servetus! Servetus! Servetus
Servetus! Servetus! Servetus! Servetus! Servetus
Servetus! Servetus! Servetus! Servetus! Servetus
Servetus! Servetus! Servetus! Servetus! Servetus
Servetus! Servetus! Servetus! Servetus! Servetus

Servetus! Servetus! Servetus! Servetus! Servetus
Servetus! Servetus! Servetus! Servetus! Servetus
Servetus! Servetus! Servetus! Servetus! Servetus
Servetus! Servetus! Servetus! Servetus! Servetus
Servetus! Servetus! Servetus! Servetus! Servetus
Servetus! Servetus! Servetus! Servetus! Servetus
Servetus! Servetus! Servetus! Servetus! Servetus
Servetus! Servetus! Servetus! Servetus! Servetus
Servetus! Servetus! Servetus! Servetus! Servetus
Servetus! Servetus! Servetus! Servetus! Servetus
Servetus! Servetus! Servetus! Servetus! Servetus
Servetus! Servetus! Servetus! Servetus! Servetus
Servetus! Servetus! Servetus! Servetus! Servetus
Servetus! Servetus! Servetus! Servetus! Servetus
Servetus! Servetus! Servetus! Servetus! Servetus
Servetus! Servetus! Servetus! Servetus! Servetus
Servetus! Servetus! Servetus! Servetus! Servetus
Servetus! Servetus! Servetus! Servetus! Servetus
Servetus! Servetus! Servetus! Servetus! Servetus
Servetus! Servetus! Servetus! Servetus! Servetus
Servetus! Servetus! Servetus! Servetus! Servetus
Servetus! Servetus! Servetus! Servetus! Servetus
Servetus! Servetus! Servetus! Servetus! Servetus
Servetus! Servetus! Servetus! Servetus! Servetus

Servetus! Servetus! Servetus! Servetus! Servetus
Servetus! Servetus! Servetus! Servetus! Servetus
Servetus! Servetus! Servetus! Servetus! Servetus
Servetus! Servetus! Servetus! Servetus! Servetus
Servetus! Servetus! Servetus! Servetus! Servetus
Servetus! Servetus! Servetus! Servetus! Servetus
Servetus! Servetus! Servetus! Servetus! Servetus
Servetus! Servetus! Servetus! Servetus! Servetus
Servetus! Servetus! Servetus! Servetus! Servetus
Servetus! Servetus! Servetus! Servetus! Servetus
Servetus! Servetus! Servetus! Servetus! Servetus
Servetus! Servetus! Servetus! Servetus! Servetus
Servetus! Servetus! Servetus! Servetus! Servetus
Servetus! Servetus! Servetus! Servetus! Servetus
Servetus! Servetus! Servetus! Servetus! Servetus
Servetus! Servetus! Servetus! Servetus! Servetus
Servetus! Servetus! Servetus! Servetus! Servetus
Servetus! Servetus! Servetus! Servetus! Servetus
Servetus! Servetus! Servetus! Servetus! Servetus
Servetus! Servetus! Servetus! Servetus! Servetus
Servetus! Servetus! Servetus! Servetus! Servetus
Servetus! Servetus! Servetus! Servetus! Servetus
Servetus! Servetus! Servetus! Servetus! Servetus
Servetus! Servetus! Servetus! Servetus! Servetus
Servetus! Servetus! Servetus! Servetus! Servetus
Servetus! Servetus! Servetus! Servetus! Servetus
Servetus! Servetus! Servetus! Servetus! Servetus
Servetus! Servetus! Servetus! Servetus! Servetus
Servetus! Servetus! Servetus! Servetus! Servetus

Servetus!	Servetus!	Servetus!	Servetus!	Servetus
Servetus!	Servetus!	Servetus!	Servetus!	Servetus
Servetus!	Servetus!	Servetus!	Servetus!	Servetus
Servetus!	Servetus!	Servetus!	Servetus!	Servetus
Servetus!	Servetus!	Servetus!	Servetus!	Servetus
Servetus!	Servetus!	Servetus!	Servetus!	Servetus
Servetus!	Servetus!	Servetus!	Servetus!	Servetus
Servetus!	Servetus!	Servetus!	Servetus!	Servetus
Servetus!	Servetus!	Servetus!	Servetus!	Servetus
Servetus!	Servetus!	Servetus!	Servetus!	Servetus
Servetus!	Servetus!	Servetus!	Servetus!	Servetus
Servetus!	Servetus!	Servetus!	Servetus!	Servetus
Servetus!	Servetus!	Servetus!	Servetus!	Servetus
Servetus!	Servetus!	Servetus!	Servetus!	Servetus
Servetus!	Servetus!	Servetus!	Servetus!	Servetus
Servetus!	Servetus!	Servetus!	Servetus!	Servetus
Servetus!	Servetus!	Servetus!	Servetus!	Servetus
Servetus!	Servetus!	Servetus!	Servetus!	Servetus
Servetus!	Servetus!	Servetus!	Servetus!	Servetus
Servetus!	Servetus!	Servetus!	Servetus!	Servetus
Servetus!	Servetus!	Servetus!	Servetus!	Servetus
Servetus!	Servetus!	Servetus!	Servetus!	Servetus
Servetus!	Servetus!	Servetus!	Servetus!	Servetus
Servetus!	Servetus!	Servetus!	Servetus!	Servetus
Servetus!	Servetus!	Servetus!	Servetus!	Servetus
Servetus!	Servetus!	Servetus!	Servetus!	Servetus
Servetus!	Servetus!	Servetus!	Servetus!	Servetus
Servetus!	Servetus!	Servetus!	Servetus!	Servetus

Servetus! Servetus! Servetus! Servetus! Servetus
Servetus! Servetus! Servetus! Servetus! Servetus
Servetus! Servetus! Servetus! Servetus! Servetus
Servetus! Servetus! Servetus! Servetus! Servetus
Servetus! Servetus! Servetus! Servetus! Servetus
Servetus! Servetus! Servetus! Servetus! Servetus
Servetus! Servetus! Servetus! Servetus! Servetus
Servetus! Servetus! Servetus! Servetus! Servetus
Servetus! Servetus! Servetus! Servetus! Servetus
Servetus! Servetus! Servetus! Servetus! Servetus
Servetus! Servetus! Servetus! Servetus! Servetus
Servetus! Servetus! Servetus! Servetus! Servetus
Servetus! Servetus! Servetus! Servetus! Servetus
Servetus! Servetus! Servetus! Servetus! Servetus
Servetus! Servetus! Servetus! Servetus! Servetus
Servetus! Servetus! Servetus! Servetus! Servetus
Servetus! Servetus! Servetus! Servetus! Servetus
Servetus! Servetus! Servetus! Servetus! Servetus
Servetus! Servetus! Servetus! Servetus! Servetus
Servetus! Servetus! Servetus! Servetus! Servetus
Servetus! Servetus! Servetus! Servetus! Servetus
Servetus! Servetus! Servetus! Servetus! Servetus
Servetus! Servetus! Servetus! Servetus! Servetus
Servetus! Servetus! Servetus! Servetus! Servetus
Servetus! Servetus! Servetus! Servetus! Servetus
Servetus! Servetus! Servetus! Servetus! Servetus
Servetus! Servetus! Servetus! Servetus! Servetus

Servetus! Servetus! Servetus! Servetus! Servetus
Servetus! Servetus! Servetus! Servetus! Servetus
Servetus! Servetus! Servetus! Servetus! Servetus
Servetus! Servetus! Servetus! Servetus! Servetus
Servetus! Servetus! Servetus! Servetus! Servetus
Servetus! Servetus! Servetus! Servetus! Servetus
Servetus! Servetus! Servetus! Servetus! Servetus
Servetus! Servetus! Servetus! Servetus! Servetus
Servetus! Servetus! Servetus! Servetus! Servetus
Servetus! Servetus! Servetus! Servetus! Servetus
Servetus! Servetus! Servetus! Servetus! Servetus
Servetus! Servetus! Servetus! Servetus! Servetus
Servetus! Servetus! Servetus! Servetus! Servetus
Servetus! Servetus! Servetus! Servetus! Servetus
Servetus! Servetus! Servetus! Servetus! Servetus
Servetus! Servetus! Servetus! Servetus! Servetus
Servetus! Servetus! Servetus! Servetus! Servetus
Servetus! Servetus! Servetus! Servetus! Servetus
Servetus! Servetus! Servetus! Servetus! Servetus
Servetus! Servetus! Servetus! Servetus! Servetus
Servetus! Servetus! Servetus! Servetus! Servetus
Servetus! Servetus! Servetus! Servetus! Servetus
Servetus! Servetus! Servetus! Servetus! Servetus
Servetus! Servetus! Servetus! Servetus! Servetus
Servetus! Servetus! Servetus! Servetus! Servetus
Servetus! Servetus! Servetus! Servetus! Servetus
Servetus! Servetus! Servetus! Servetus! Servetus
Servetus! Servetus! Servetus! Servetus! Servetus

Servetus! Servetus! Servetus! Servetus! Servetus
Servetus! Servetus! Servetus! Servetus! Servetus
Servetus! Servetus! Servetus! Servetus! Servetus
Servetus! Servetus! Servetus! Servetus! Servetus
Servetus! Servetus! Servetus! Servetus! Servetus
Servetus! Servetus! Servetus! Servetus! Servetus
Servetus! Servetus! Servetus! Servetus! Servetus
Servetus! Servetus! Servetus! Servetus! Servetus
Servetus! Servetus! Servetus! Servetus! Servetus
Servetus! Servetus! Servetus! Servetus! Servetus
Servetus! Servetus! Servetus! Servetus! Servetus
Servetus! Servetus! Servetus! Servetus! Servetus
Servetus! Servetus! Servetus! Servetus! Servetus
Servetus! Servetus! Servetus! Servetus! Servetus
Servetus! Servetus! Servetus! Servetus! Servetus
Servetus! Servetus! Servetus! Servetus! Servetus
Servetus! Servetus! Servetus! Servetus! Servetus
Servetus! Servetus! Servetus! Servetus! Servetus
Servetus! Servetus! Servetus! Servetus! Servetus
Servetus! Servetus! Servetus! Servetus! Servetus
Servetus! Servetus! Servetus! Servetus! Servetus
Servetus! Servetus! Servetus! Servetus! Servetus
Servetus! Servetus! Servetus! Servetus! Servetus
Servetus! Servetus! Servetus! Servetus! Servetus
Servetus! Servetus! Servetus! Servetus! Servetus
Servetus! Servetus! Servetus! Servetus! Servetus
Servetus! Servetus! Servetus! Servetus! Servetus
Servetus! Servetus! Servetus! Servetus! Servetus

Servetus! Servetus! Servetus! Servetus! Servetus
Servetus! Servetus! Servetus! Servetus! Servetus
Servetus! Servetus! Servetus! Servetus! Servetus
Servetus! Servetus! Servetus! Servetus! Servetus
Servetus! Servetus! Servetus! Servetus! Servetus
Servetus! Servetus! Servetus! Servetus! Servetus
Servetus! Servetus! Servetus! Servetus! Servetus
Servetus! Servetus! Servetus! Servetus! Servetus
Servetus! Servetus! Servetus! Servetus! Servetus
Servetus! Servetus! Servetus! Servetus! Servetus
Servetus! Servetus! Servetus! Servetus! Servetus
Servetus! Servetus! Servetus! Servetus! Servetus
Servetus! Servetus! Servetus! Servetus! Servetus
Servetus! Servetus! Servetus! Servetus! Servetus
Servetus! Servetus! Servetus! Servetus! Servetus
Servetus! Servetus! Servetus! Servetus! Servetus
Servetus! Servetus! Servetus! Servetus! Servetus
Servetus! Servetus! Servetus! Servetus! Servetus
Servetus! Servetus! Servetus! Servetus! Servetus
Servetus! Servetus! Servetus! Servetus! Servetus
Servetus! Servetus! Servetus! Servetus! Servetus
Servetus! Servetus! Servetus! Servetus! Servetus
Servetus! Servetus! Servetus! Servetus! Servetus
Servetus! Servetus! Servetus! Servetus! Servetus
Servetus! Servetus! Servetus! Servetus! Servetus
Servetus! Servetus! Servetus! Servetus! Servetus
Servetus! Servetus! Servetus! Servetus! Servetus
Servetus! Servetus! Servetus! Servetus! Servetus
Servetus! Servetus! Servetus! Servetus! Servetus

Servetus! Servetus! Servetus! Servetus! Servetus
Servetus! Servetus! Servetus! Servetus! Servetus
Servetus! Servetus! Servetus! Servetus! Servetus
Servetus! Servetus! Servetus! Servetus! Servetus
Servetus! Servetus! Servetus! Servetus! Servetus
Servetus! Servetus! Servetus! Servetus! Servetus
Servetus! Servetus! Servetus! Servetus! Servetus
Servetus! Servetus! Servetus! Servetus! Servetus
Servetus! Servetus! Servetus! Servetus! Servetus
Servetus! Servetus! Servetus! Servetus! Servetus
Servetus! Servetus! Servetus! Servetus! Servetus
Servetus! Servetus! Servetus! Servetus! Servetus
Servetus! Servetus! Servetus! Servetus! Servetus
Servetus! Servetus! Servetus! Servetus! Servetus
Servetus! Servetus! Servetus! Servetus! Servetus
Servetus! Servetus! Servetus! Servetus! Servetus
Servetus! Servetus! Servetus! Servetus! Servetus
Servetus! Servetus! Servetus! Servetus! Servetus
Servetus! Servetus! Servetus! Servetus! Servetus
Servetus! Servetus! Servetus! Servetus! Servetus
Servetus! Servetus! Servetus! Servetus! Servetus
Servetus! Servetus! Servetus! Servetus! Servetus
Servetus! Servetus! Servetus! Servetus! Servetus
Servetus! Servetus! Servetus! Servetus! Servetus
Servetus! Servetus! Servetus! Servetus! Servetus
Servetus! Servetus! Servetus! Servetus! Servetus
Servetus! Servetus! Servetus! Servetus! Servetus

Please Stop Saying "Romans 9"

Nations! Nations! Nations! Nations! Nations!
Nations! Nations! Nations! Nations! Nations!
Nations! Nations! Nations! Nations! Nations!
Nations! Nations! Nations! Nations! Nations!
Nations! Nations! Nations! Nations! Nations!
Nations! Nations! Nations! Nations! Nations!
Nations! Nations! Nations! Nations! Nations!
Nations! Nations! Nations! Nations! Nations!
Nations! Nations! Nations! Nations! Nations!
Nations! Nations! Nations! Nations! Nations!
Nations! Nations! Nations! Nations! Nations!
Nations! Nations! Nations! Nations! Nations!
Nations! Nations! Nations! Nations! Nations!
Nations! Nations! Nations! Nations! Nations!
Nations! Nations! Nations! Nations! Nations!
Nations! Nations! Nations! Nations! Nations!
Nations! Nations! Nations! Nations! Nations!
Nations! Nations! Nations! Nations! Nations!
Nations! Nations! Nations! Nations! Nations!
Nations! Nations! Nations! Nations! Nations!
Nations! Nations! Nations! Nations! Nations!
Nations! Nations! Nations! Nations! Nations!
Nations! Nations! Nations! Nations! Nations!
Nations! Nations! Nations! Nations! Nations!
Nations! Nations! Nations! Nations! Nations!

Nations! Nations! Nations! Nations! Nations!
Nations! Nations! Nations! Nations! Nations!
Nations! Nations! Nations! Nations! Nations!
Nations! Nations! Nations! Nations! Nations!
Nations! Nations! Nations! Nations! Nations!
Nations! Nations! Nations! Nations! Nations!
Nations! Nations! Nations! Nations! Nations!
Nations! Nations! Nations! Nations! Nations!
Nations! Nations! Nations! Nations! Nations!
Nations! Nations! Nations! Nations! Nations!
Nations! Nations! Nations! Nations! Nations!
Nations! Nations! Nations! Nations! Nations!
Nations! Nations! Nations! Nations! Nations!
Nations! Nations! Nations! Nations! Nations!
Nations! Nations! Nations! Nations! Nations!
Nations! Nations! Nations! Nations! Nations!
Nations! Nations! Nations! Nations! Nations!
Nations! Nations! Nations! Nations! Nations!
Nations! Nations! Nations! Nations! Nations!
Nations! Nations! Nations! Nations! Nations!
Nations! Nations! Nations! Nations! Nations!
Nations! Nations! Nations! Nations! Nations!
Nations! Nations! Nations! Nations! Nations!
Nations! Nations! Nations! Nations! Nations!
Nations! Nations! Nations! Nations! Nations!
Nations! Nations! Nations! Nations! Nations!

Nations! Nations! Nations! Nations! Nations!
Nations! Nations! Nations! Nations! Nations!
Nations! Nations! Nations! Nations! Nations!
Nations! Nations! Nations! Nations! Nations!
Nations! Nations! Nations! Nations! Nations!
Nations! Nations! Nations! Nations! Nations!
Nations! Nations! Nations! Nations! Nations!
Nations! Nations! Nations! Nations! Nations!
Nations! Nations! Nations! Nations! Nations!
Nations! Nations! Nations! Nations! Nations!
Nations! Nations! Nations! Nations! Nations!
Nations! Nations! Nations! Nations! Nations!
Nations! Nations! Nations! Nations! Nations!
Nations! Nations! Nations! Nations! Nations!
Nations! Nations! Nations! Nations! Nations!
Nations! Nations! Nations! Nations! Nations!
Nations! Nations! Nations! Nations! Nations!
Nations! Nations! Nations! Nations! Nations!
Nations! Nations! Nations! Nations! Nations!
Nations! Nations! Nations! Nations! Nations!
Nations! Nations! Nations! Nations! Nations!
Nations! Nations! Nations! Nations! Nations!
Nations! Nations! Nations! Nations! Nations!
Nations! Nations! Nations! Nations! Nations!
Nations! Nations! Nations! Nations! Nations!
Nations! Nations! Nations! Nations! Nations!
Nations! Nations! Nations! Nations! Nations!
Nations! Nations! Nations! Nations! Nations!

Nations! Nations! Nations! Nations! Nations!
Nations! Nations! Nations! Nations! Nations!
Nations! Nations! Nations! Nations! Nations!
Nations! Nations! Nations! Nations! Nations!
Nations! Nations! Nations! Nations! Nations!
Nations! Nations! Nations! Nations! Nations!
Nations! Nations! Nations! Nations! Nations!
Nations! Nations! Nations! Nations! Nations!
Nations! Nations! Nations! Nations! Nations!
Nations! Nations! Nations! Nations! Nations!
Nations! Nations! Nations! Nations! Nations!
Nations! Nations! Nations! Nations! Nations!
Nations! Nations! Nations! Nations! Nations!
Nations! Nations! Nations! Nations! Nations!
Nations! Nations! Nations! Nations! Nations!
Nations! Nations! Nations! Nations! Nations!
Nations! Nations! Nations! Nations! Nations!
Nations! Nations! Nations! Nations! Nations!
Nations! Nations! Nations! Nations! Nations!
Nations! Nations! Nations! Nations! Nations!
Nations! Nations! Nations! Nations! Nations!
Nations! Nations! Nations! Nations! Nations!
Nations! Nations! Nations! Nations! Nations!
Nations! Nations! Nations! Nations! Nations!
Nations! Nations! Nations! Nations! Nations!

Nations! Nations! Nations! Nations! Nations!
Nations! Nations! Nations! Nations! Nations!
Nations! Nations! Nations! Nations! Nations!
Nations! Nations! Nations! Nations! Nations!
Nations! Nations! Nations! Nations! Nations!
Nations! Nations! Nations! Nations! Nations!
Nations! Nations! Nations! Nations! Nations!
Nations! Nations! Nations! Nations! Nations!
Nations! Nations! Nations! Nations! Nations!
Nations! Nations! Nations! Nations! Nations!
Nations! Nations! Nations! Nations! Nations!
Nations! Nations! Nations! Nations! Nations!
Nations! Nations! Nations! Nations! Nations!
Nations! Nations! Nations! Nations! Nations!
Nations! Nations! Nations! Nations! Nations!
Nations! Nations! Nations! Nations! Nations!
Nations! Nations! Nations! Nations! Nations!
Nations! Nations! Nations! Nations! Nations!
Nations! Nations! Nations! Nations! Nations!
Nations! Nations! Nations! Nations! Nations!
Nations! Nations! Nations! Nations! Nations!
Nations! Nations! Nations! Nations! Nations!
Nations! Nations! Nations! Nations! Nations!
Nations! Nations! Nations! Nations! Nations!

Nations! Nations! Nations! Nations! Nations!
Nations! Nations! Nations! Nations! Nations!
Nations! Nations! Nations! Nations! Nations!
Nations! Nations! Nations! Nations! Nations!
Nations! Nations! Nations! Nations! Nations!
Nations! Nations! Nations! Nations! Nations!
Nations! Nations! Nations! Nations! Nations!
Nations! Nations! Nations! Nations! Nations!
Nations! Nations! Nations! Nations! Nations!
Nations! Nations! Nations! Nations! Nations!
Nations! Nations! Nations! Nations! Nations!
Nations! Nations! Nations! Nations! Nations!
Nations! Nations! Nations! Nations! Nations!
Nations! Nations! Nations! Nations! Nations!
Nations! Nations! Nations! Nations! Nations!
Nations! Nations! Nations! Nations! Nations!
Nations! Nations! Nations! Nations! Nations!
Nations! Nations! Nations! Nations! Nations!
Nations! Nations! Nations! Nations! Nations!
Nations! Nations! Nations! Nations! Nations!
Nations! Nations! Nations! Nations! Nations!
Nations! Nations! Nations! Nations! Nations!
Nations! Nations! Nations! Nations! Nations!
Nations! Nations! Nations! Nations! Nations!
Nations! Nations! Nations! Nations! Nations!

Nations! Nations! Nations! Nations! Nations!
Nations! Nations! Nations! Nations! Nations!
Nations! Nations! Nations! Nations! Nations!
Nations! Nations! Nations! Nations! Nations!
Nations! Nations! Nations! Nations! Nations!
Nations! Nations! Nations! Nations! Nations!
Nations! Nations! Nations! Nations! Nations!
Nations! Nations! Nations! Nations! Nations!
Nations! Nations! Nations! Nations! Nations!
Nations! Nations! Nations! Nations! Nations!
Nations! Nations! Nations! Nations! Nations!
Nations! Nations! Nations! Nations! Nations!
Nations! Nations! Nations! Nations! Nations!
Nations! Nations! Nations! Nations! Nations!
Nations! Nations! Nations! Nations! Nations!
Nations! Nations! Nations! Nations! Nations!
Nations! Nations! Nations! Nations! Nations!
Nations! Nations! Nations! Nations! Nations!
Nations! Nations! Nations! Nations! Nations!
Nations! Nations! Nations! Nations! Nations!
Nations! Nations! Nations! Nations! Nations!
Nations! Nations! Nations! Nations! Nations!
Nations! Nations! Nations! Nations! Nations!
Nations! Nations! Nations! Nations! Nations!
Nations! Nations! Nations! Nations! Nations!
Nations! Nations! Nations! Nations! Nations!
Nations! Nations! Nations! Nations! Nations!
Nations! Nations! Nations! Nations! Nations!

Nations! Nations! Nations! Nations! Nations!
Nations! Nations! Nations! Nations! Nations!
Nations! Nations! Nations! Nations! Nations!
Nations! Nations! Nations! Nations! Nations!
Nations! Nations! Nations! Nations! Nations!
Nations! Nations! Nations! Nations! Nations!
Nations! Nations! Nations! Nations! Nations!
Nations! Nations! Nations! Nations! Nations!
Nations! Nations! Nations! Nations! Nations!
Nations! Nations! Nations! Nations! Nations!
Nations! Nations! Nations! Nations! Nations!
Nations! Nations! Nations! Nations! Nations!
Nations! Nations! Nations! Nations! Nations!
Nations! Nations! Nations! Nations! Nations!
Nations! Nations! Nations! Nations! Nations!
Nations! Nations! Nations! Nations! Nations!
Nations! Nations! Nations! Nations! Nations!
Nations! Nations! Nations! Nations! Nations!
Nations! Nations! Nations! Nations! Nations!
Nations! Nations! Nations! Nations! Nations!
Nations! Nations! Nations! Nations! Nations!
Nations! Nations! Nations! Nations! Nations!
Nations! Nations! Nations! Nations! Nations!
Nations! Nations! Nations! Nations! Nations!
Nations! Nations! Nations! Nations! Nations!

Nations! Nations! Nations! Nations! Nations!
Nations! Nations! Nations! Nations! Nations!
Nations! Nations! Nations! Nations! Nations!
Nations! Nations! Nations! Nations! Nations!
Nations! Nations! Nations! Nations! Nations!
Nations! Nations! Nations! Nations! Nations!
Nations! Nations! Nations! Nations! Nations!
Nations! Nations! Nations! Nations! Nations!
Nations! Nations! Nations! Nations! Nations!
Nations! Nations! Nations! Nations! Nations!
Nations! Nations! Nations! Nations! Nations!
Nations! Nations! Nations! Nations! Nations!
Nations! Nations! Nations! Nations! Nations!
Nations! Nations! Nations! Nations! Nations!
Nations! Nations! Nations! Nations! Nations!
Nations! Nations! Nations! Nations! Nations!
Nations! Nations! Nations! Nations! Nations!
Nations! Nations! Nations! Nations! Nations!
Nations! Nations! Nations! Nations! Nations!
Nations! Nations! Nations! Nations! Nations!
Nations! Nations! Nations! Nations! Nations!
Nations! Nations! Nations! Nations! Nations!
Nations! Nations! Nations! Nations! Nations!
Nations! Nations! Nations! Nations! Nations!
Nations! Nations! Nations! Nations! Nations!

Nations! Nations! Nations! Nations! Nations!
Nations! Nations! Nations! Nations! Nations!
Nations! Nations! Nations! Nations! Nations!
Nations! Nations! Nations! Nations! Nations!
Nations! Nations! Nations! Nations! Nations!
Nations! Nations! Nations! Nations! Nations!
Nations! Nations! Nations! Nations! Nations!
Nations! Nations! Nations! Nations! Nations!
Nations! Nations! Nations! Nations! Nations!
Nations! Nations! Nations! Nations! Nations!
Nations! Nations! Nations! Nations! Nations!
Nations! Nations! Nations! Nations! Nations!
Nations! Nations! Nations! Nations! Nations!
Nations! Nations! Nations! Nations! Nations!
Nations! Nations! Nations! Nations! Nations!
Nations! Nations! Nations! Nations! Nations!
Nations! Nations! Nations! Nations! Nations!
Nations! Nations! Nations! Nations! Nations!
Nations! Nations! Nations! Nations! Nations!
Nations! Nations! Nations! Nations! Nations!
Nations! Nations! Nations! Nations! Nations!
Nations! Nations! Nations! Nations! Nations!
Nations! Nations! Nations! Nations! Nations!

Nations! Nations! Nations! Nations! Nations!
Nations! Nations! Nations! Nations! Nations!
Nations! Nations! Nations! Nations! Nations!
Nations! Nations! Nations! Nations! Nations!
Nations! Nations! Nations! Nations! Nations!
Nations! Nations! Nations! Nations! Nations!
Nations! Nations! Nations! Nations! Nations!
Nations! Nations! Nations! Nations! Nations!
Nations! Nations! Nations! Nations! Nations!
Nations! Nations! Nations! Nations! Nations!
Nations! Nations! Nations! Nations! Nations!
Nations! Nations! Nations! Nations! Nations!
Nations! Nations! Nations! Nations! Nations!
Nations! Nations! Nations! Nations! Nations!
Nations! Nations! Nations! Nations! Nations!
Nations! Nations! Nations! Nations! Nations!
Nations! Nations! Nations! Nations! Nations!
Nations! Nations! Nations! Nations! Nations!
Nations! Nations! Nations! Nations! Nations!
Nations! Nations! Nations! Nations! Nations!
Nations! Nations! Nations! Nations! Nations!
Nations! Nations! Nations! Nations! Nations!
Nations! Nations! Nations! Nations! Nations!
Nations! Nations! Nations! Nations! Nations!
Nations! Nations! Nations! Nations! Nations!

Nations! Nations! Nations! Nations! Nations!
Nations! Nations! Nations! Nations! Nations!
Nations! Nations! Nations! Nations! Nations!
Nations! Nations! Nations! Nations! Nations!
Nations! Nations! Nations! Nations! Nations!
Nations! Nations! Nations! Nations! Nations!
Nations! Nations! Nations! Nations! Nations!
Nations! Nations! Nations! Nations! Nations!
Nations! Nations! Nations! Nations! Nations!
Nations! Nations! Nations! Nations! Nations!
Nations! Nations! Nations! Nations! Nations!
Nations! Nations! Nations! Nations! Nations!
Nations! Nations! Nations! Nations! Nations!
Nations! Nations! Nations! Nations! Nations!
Nations! Nations! Nations! Nations! Nations!
Nations! Nations! Nations! Nations! Nations!
Nations! Nations! Nations! Nations! Nations!
Nations! Nations! Nations! Nations! Nations!
Nations! Nations! Nations! Nations! Nations!
Nations! Nations! Nations! Nations! Nations!
Nations! Nations! Nations! Nations! Nations!
Nations! Nations! Nations! Nations! Nations!
Nations! Nations! Nations! Nations! Nations!
Nations! Nations! Nations! Nations! Nations!
Nations! Nations! Nations! Nations! Nations!
Nations! Nations! Nations! Nations! Nations!
Nations! Nations! Nations! Nations! Nations!

Nations! Nations! Nations! Nations! Nations!
Nations! Nations! Nations! Nations! Nations!
Nations! Nations! Nations! Nations! Nations!
Nations! Nations! Nations! Nations! Nations!
Nations! Nations! Nations! Nations! Nations!
Nations! Nations! Nations! Nations! Nations!
Nations! Nations! Nations! Nations! Nations!
Nations! Nations! Nations! Nations! Nations!
Nations! Nations! Nations! Nations! Nations!
Nations! Nations! Nations! Nations! Nations!
Nations! Nations! Nations! Nations! Nations!
Nations! Nations! Nations! Nations! Nations!
Nations! Nations! Nations! Nations! Nations!
Nations! Nations! Nations! Nations! Nations!
Nations! Nations! Nations! Nations! Nations!
Nations! Nations! Nations! Nations! Nations!
Nations! Nations! Nations! Nations! Nations!
Nations! Nations! Nations! Nations! Nations!
Nations! Nations! Nations! Nations! Nations!
Nations! Nations! Nations! Nations! Nations!
Nations! Nations! Nations! Nations! Nations!
Nations! Nations! Nations! Nations! Nations!
Nations! Nations! Nations! Nations! Nations!
Nations! Nations! Nations! Nations! Nations!
Nations! Nations! Nations! Nations! Nations!

Nations! Nations! Nations! Nations! Nations!
Nations! Nations! Nations! Nations! Nations!
Nations! Nations! Nations! Nations! Nations!
Nations! Nations! Nations! Nations! Nations!
Nations! Nations! Nations! Nations! Nations!
Nations! Nations! Nations! Nations! Nations!
Nations! Nations! Nations! Nations! Nations!
Nations! Nations! Nations! Nations! Nations!
Nations! Nations! Nations! Nations! Nations!
Nations! Nations! Nations! Nations! Nations!
Nations! Nations! Nations! Nations! Nations!
Nations! Nations! Nations! Nations! Nations!
Nations! Nations! Nations! Nations! Nations!
Nations! Nations! Nations! Nations! Nations!
Nations! Nations! Nations! Nations! Nations!
Nations! Nations! Nations! Nations! Nations!
Nations! Nations! Nations! Nations! Nations!
Nations! Nations! Nations! Nations! Nations!
Nations! Nations! Nations! Nations! Nations!
Nations! Nations! Nations! Nations! Nations!
Nations! Nations! Nations! Nations! Nations!
Nations! Nations! Nations! Nations! Nations!
Nations! Nations! Nations! Nations! Nations!
Nations! Nations! Nations! Nations! Nations!
Nations! Nations! Nations! Nations! Nations!

Nations! Nations! Nations! Nations! Nations!
Nations! Nations! Nations! Nations! Nations!
Nations! Nations! Nations! Nations! Nations!
Nations! Nations! Nations! Nations! Nations!
Nations! Nations! Nations! Nations! Nations!
Nations! Nations! Nations! Nations! Nations!
Nations! Nations! Nations! Nations! Nations!
Nations! Nations! Nations! Nations! Nations!
Nations! Nations! Nations! Nations! Nations!
Nations! Nations! Nations! Nations! Nations!
Nations! Nations! Nations! Nations! Nations!
Nations! Nations! Nations! Nations! Nations!
Nations! Nations! Nations! Nations! Nations!
Nations! Nations! Nations! Nations! Nations!
Nations! Nations! Nations! Nations! Nations!
Nations! Nations! Nations! Nations! Nations!
Nations! Nations! Nations! Nations! Nations!
Nations! Nations! Nations! Nations! Nations!
Nations! Nations! Nations! Nations! Nations!
Nations! Nations! Nations! Nations! Nations!
Nations! Nations! Nations! Nations! Nations!
Nations! Nations! Nations! Nations! Nations!
Nations! Nations! Nations! Nations! Nations!
Nations! Nations! Nations! Nations! Nations!
Nations! Nations! Nations! Nations! Nations!
Nations! Nations! Nations! Nations! Nations!

Nations! Nations! Nations! Nations! Nations!
Nations! Nations! Nations! Nations! Nations!
Nations! Nations! Nations! Nations! Nations!
Nations! Nations! Nations! Nations! Nations!
Nations! Nations! Nations! Nations! Nations!
Nations! Nations! Nations! Nations! Nations!
Nations! Nations! Nations! Nations! Nations!
Nations! Nations! Nations! Nations! Nations!
Nations! Nations! Nations! Nations! Nations!
Nations! Nations! Nations! Nations! Nations!
Nations! Nations! Nations! Nations! Nations!
Nations! Nations! Nations! Nations! Nations!
Nations! Nations! Nations! Nations! Nations!
Nations! Nations! Nations! Nations! Nations!
Nations! Nations! Nations! Nations! Nations!
Nations! Nations! Nations! Nations! Nations!
Nations! Nations! Nations! Nations! Nations!
Nations! Nations! Nations! Nations! Nations!
Nations! Nations! Nations! Nations! Nations!
Nations! Nations! Nations! Nations! Nations!
Nations! Nations! Nations! Nations! Nations!
Nations! Nations! Nations! Nations! Nations!
Nations! Nations! Nations! Nations! Nations!

The End ;)

www.ingramcontent.com/pod-product-compliance
Lightning Source LLC
Chambersburg PA
CBHW062042280526
45788CB00003B/1085